Charles Wendel
Colson

Oct. 16, 1931 –

WOMEN OF FAITH SERIES

Amy Carmichael
Corrie ten Boom
Florence Nightingale
Gladys Aylward
Hannah Whitall Smith
Isobel Kuhn
Joni
Mary Slessor

MEN OF FAITH SERIES

Borden of Yale
Brother Andrew
C. S. Lewis
Charles Colson
Charles Finney
Charles Spurgeon
D. L. Moody
Eric Liddell
George Muller
Hudson Taylor
Jim Elliot
Jonathan Goforth
John Hyde
John Newton
John Wesley
Martin Luther
Samuel Morris
Terry Waite
William Carey
William Booth

John and Betty Stam

Charles Colson

Stella Wiseman

BETHANY HOUSE PUBLISHERS
MINNEAPOLIS, MINNESOTA 55438

Originally published in England by Marshall Pickering, an imprint of HarperCollins Publishing, Ltd., under the title *Charles Colson* ©1995 Stella Wiseman.

The author asserts the moral right to be indentified as the author of this work.

Cover by Dan Thornberg,
Bethany House Publishers staff artist.

Published by Bethany House Publishers
A Ministry of Bethany Fellowship, Inc.
11300 Hampshire Avenue South
Minneapolis, Minnesota 55438

Printed in the United States of America.

Library of Congress Cataloging-in-Publication Data

Wiseman, Stella.
    Charles Colson / Stella Wiseman.
       p. cm.

    1. Colson, Charles W. 2. Baptists—United States—
Biography. 3. Evangelists—United States—Biography.
4. Ex-convicts—United States—Biography. 5. Prison
Fellowship—Biography. I. Title. II. Series.
BX6495.C5687W57   1995
286'.1'092—dc20
[B]   95–6182
ISBN 1–55661–629–5   CIP

Contents

Scenes from a Life

Charles Colson and his father gazed out over the Rose Garden at the White House. The peace was soothing after the noise of the ceremony they had just left, where President Nixon had awarded medals to some Vietnam veterans. Charles's father Wendell felt a little dazed by the splendour, by the military bands, the television cameras and above all by the presence of arguably the most powerful man in the world, the American President himself.

As they stood there they heard the sound of running feet. A White House official rushed up to them. 'Mr Colson,' he said, addressing Wendell, 'the President would like to see you.'

The minutes that followed were among the proudest in Wendell Colson's life. President Nixon invited the Colsons, father and son, into the Oval Office in the heart of the White House and talked with Wendell, a lifetime Republican supporter. The White House photographer was called and took a picture of the three of them. Then the President said something that made Wendell almost burst with pride: 'I rely so much on your son Chuck's advice.'

* * * * * *

The unmarked car raced through the streets of Baltimore, leaving the press far behind. Squashed in the back seat, Chuck looked forlornly out at the dirty streets. They passed through some gates and drove past empty, soot-covered buildings with boarded-up windows, surrounded by overgrown grass and trees. Everywhere was deserted.

The car stopped in front of the one building which showed signs of life, an ugly green construction surrounded by a nine-foot-high chain link fence topped with jagged barbed wire. Two armed guards stepped forward and opened the tall gate in the fence and the men in the car with Chuck motioned to him to get out. With one man on either side, Chuck walked through the open gateway. It slammed behind him with a decisive crash. Chuck Colson was a convicted criminal.

* * * * * *

The room was cool enough that day in early May, but a little bead of sweat formed on Chuck's brow. He had once walked the corridors of power in Washington, he had visited many countries, met many dignitaries and had received a number of awards and honorary degrees from universities. Here, however, in this splendid room, he felt more than a little daunted.

He could hear a voice speaking. It was talking about him: praising him for his vision, his courage and his work. 'Occasions like this,' thought Chuck, 'could make me proud. I must hold on to the fact that I could have done none of this without God.'

The voice stopped and Chuck stepped forward. He put out his hand and Prince Philip, the Duke of Edinburgh, clasped it in his own, then presented him with a cheque for £650,000. That day at Buckingham Palace Chuck Colson became the 1993 recipient of the coveted Templeton Prize for Progress in Religion.

Charles Colson's life has been one of contrasts – he rose to the top in politics, suffered the ignominy of imprisonment – for a crime he certainly *did* commit – but, through the grace of God, he has become a highly respected, dynamic citizen again. Only this time, he is not giving his all to a powerful government, but bringing hope and comfort to men and women whom society likes to ignore – prisoners.

CHAPTER ONE

Pride and Patriotism

Charles Colson rounded the corner and set off up the road to his home. He approached the old Victorian house cheerfully, looking forward to the evening at home after school. Chuck, as he was known, climbed the stairs to his parents' rented apartment, turned the door handle and called 'I'm ho . . .' Chuck stopped, his words unfinished, but his mouth stayed open in astonishment. Coming out of the living room was a man carrying a chair. Behind him Chuck could see another man, stooping to pick up a second chair, a chair that belonged to the family. Chuck gasped. He knew they could not be burglars because there was his mother, watching anxiously as the men made their way across the hall and out of the door. Beside her on the table in the now barely furnished living room was a pile of dollar bills. She was selling some of the furniture to make ends meet.

Chuck was born on 16 October 1931 in a time of economic depression. The world economy had slumped at the end of the 1920s and in the 1930s unemployment was high and poverty widespread. The Colsons lived quite well, in comparison with many, in the small town of Winthrop just north across the harbour from Boston. Chuck's father Wendell was a lawyer, but he struggled to bring in enough for the family to live on. His wife Inez, however, spent whatever it took to ensure that the family was comfortable and to give their son a good education. As a result they were usually a little in debt. Sometimes, however, creditors demanded payment or the bills piled higher than usual and Inez would take action. She would sell some of the family's furniture and other possessions. That day, as Chuck watched complete strangers carrying away parts of the family home, he felt a shiver of insecurity. He did not want to live like this.

Wendell Colson worked hard. He had shown promise at high school, but tragedy struck his family and he had to leave school early, before taking his diploma. Shortly after the First World War ended in 1918 there was a massive worldwide outbreak of influenza which killed thousands of men, women and children, weakened by the war. The war killed 53,000 US troops, but by its end more people had died of the flu epidemic. Among the dead was Chuck's grandfather. Wendell left school to find a job to support his mother and sister. Later he met and married Inez Ducrow and decided to go to night school to catch up with his education and gain some more qualifications.

For twelve long, hard years he worked as a bookkeeper in a meat-packing plant, earning just $32 a week. In the evenings he went to night school and studied accounting and then law. The eight-year-old Chuck watched him graduate from Northeastern Law School. As Chuck saw his father cross the stage in his black cap and gown he felt a real pride. His dad was the best.

With all his work Chuck's father did not have a lot of time to spare, but he made sure he had time to talk to his son. Of the many things they talked about, one stuck in Chuck's mind, not just as a child but years later too: it was the need to work hard and do everything as well as possible. He also impressed on Chuck the importance of telling the truth.

For all his hard work and honesty, bad luck seemed to dog Chuck's father. Once he had his degree he did well at his business, now working for General Foods who had taken over the meat-packing plant. But his health was poor and he was forced to leave his job. He set up in practice as a lawyer on his own but, although he was a good lawyer, it was hard to be successful when most of the well-paid cases went to lawyers who had studied at Harvard.

Harvard was the university to go to if you wanted to succeed and Wendell would have been proud if his own son had gone there. Inez and Wendell were determined that Chuck should have a good education and struggled to send him to a small private school, Browne and Nichols, less than a mile from Harvard itself. Chuck worked hard there, and every summer from the age of eleven took a job to help pay the fees for the following year. By the time he graduated in 1949 he had become editor of the school newspaper and had passed his exams with honours. Every year the graduating class would vote for the student who was most likely to succeed and that year Chuck had won the vote. If any of the class were Harvard-bound, Chuck must have been top of the list. But he needed a scholarship to afford it.

Chuck applied for a scholarship at both Harvard and Brown Universities. Brown was viewed as rather second-best compared with Harvard, but they quickly offered him a scholarship. The Brown offer was of a Navy Reserve Officer Training Corps scholarship, which entitled him to tuition fees and $50 a month to live on. Then, early in June, he received a letter from Harvard. Nervously he read the words: 'Please attend an interview with the Dean of Admissions.'

A short while later, and dressed in his best, Chuck waited in the Harvard administrative building. He could feel the sense of history there: in peaceful Harvard Yard, in the antique brass in the Dean's office, in the shelves crammed with old photographs and books about Harvard, in the musty air. All around him was the atmosphere of two centuries of learning, of the best education, of students who had gone on to make their mark on America. This was the place of the élite.

The Dean greeted him, then solemnly told him that he had been awarded a full scholarship at Harvard. Chuck's heart pounded. He had done it! He felt elated and proud. But he also felt something else – resentment. His father had struggled in his law practice because of Harvard graduates' grip on Boston. For years, too, Chuck had been aware of how superior Harvard was, how it looked down on those who came from less privileged backgrounds. Suddenly he was not sure he wanted to go there.

The Dean waited, watching Chuck, expecting him to ask questions about life at Harvard, where he would live, what exactly he would study, all the usual questions that most new students asked. But Chuck was not like most students. Taking a deep breath he told the Dean that he was not sure whether he would accept a place at Harvard. Chuck may have been given the chance to join the élite, but he also had the chance to turn them down. In September 1949 Chuck arrived at university – Brown University on Rhode Island.

The Korean War was raging while Chuck was at Brown. On 25 June 1950 forces from communist North Korea invaded South Korea while the government was supported by the United States of America. The following day US President Harry Truman sent American troops in to fight the communist army and defend the South. Over the next three years more and more troops were needed to join up. When Chuck was in his second year at Brown there was a recruiting campaign on his campus, calling students to join the US Marine Corps. Chuck was fervently patriotic and decided to join up. There was, however, an obstacle he was not expecting.

The first step was to present himself before a recruiting officer. He approached First-Lieutenant Cosgrove, a graduate of the Naval Academy, and announced that he would like to join the Marines. Cosgrove stared at him. He did not look very friendly to Chuck, nor was he very impressed. In fact, he told Chuck that he would have to see if he was 'good enough' for the Marine Corps. Chuck was stunned. Of course he was good enough. His pride was hurt and he marched out of the office determined to show Cosgrove that he *was* 'good enough'.

Once a week all the Navy ROTC students wore uniforms to class and attended drill sessions in the afternoon. Cosgrove used to watch those sessions and he soon began to watch Chuck carefully. Chuck's shoes were so shiny they reflected his face; his brass was polished to perfection. What was more, Chuck obviously knew every step of the drill. Chuck even seemed to be walking like Cosgrove, with ramrod straight back and chin tucked well in. Cosgrove was impressed, which was just what Chuck had planned.

One spring day Chuck checked the notice board and saw a typewritten note addressed to him. It was a summons to First-Lieutenant Cosgrove's office. Chuck gulped. He suddenly realized that he had never really been sure that he wanted to join the Marine Corps. He had simply wanted to prove that he was 'good enough'. Now Cosgrove thought he was.

If he had any initial doubts about joining the Marines, they were soon dispelled. Chuck was proud of being a marine. As usual, he put his full effort into his work and was at one time an acting company commander, the youngest in the Marines. Although he would have done well enough on his own, he was inspired by General Puller who led Chuck's division. Puller had won the Navy Cross a record five times, and the marines loved and respected him. Above all he taught Chuck that when someone puts everything into it, he or she can achieve what seems to be impossible.

Chuck graduated from Brown in 1953 just as the Korean War ended, but he remained in the Marines.

In the summer of 1954 the young Chuck and his platoon of forty-five men received an order: to report to base to respond to an emergency. The platoon were to be sent to Guatemala in Central America to defend the lives of Americans caught in the Guatemalan communist uprising. They set sail in USS Mellette, an old ship which had seen service in the Second World War.

Late that night Chuck stood on the deck of the USS Mellette. It was a hot, sultry night. The sea was calm and the sky was clear. Around him he could see the lights of other ships in the task force. Chuck felt a weight of responsibility on him as he thought of the days to come and the lives of the forty-five men who were dependent on his command. There would be fighting, danger, possibly death, for him and for his men. Chuck stared up at the sky and the thousands of stars above him. He suddenly felt small and insignificant. He may have been important to his men, to his family and his friends, but, he thought, he was nothing more than a tiny dot, and the ship was just another slightly larger dot. The sea, vast and dark around him, also seemed small and insignificant in the endless universe.

As he stood there Chuck felt a calming certainty. Whatever happened he suddenly knew, without a doubt, there was a God, a God beyond the vastness, a God who ruled it all. Chuck had never been particularly interested in religion, but now he started to pray; stumbling a little, and uncertain whether God had the time to hear him, but certain that there was a God to pray to.

A few hours later the message came through: the

emergency was over. The communists had been beaten and the task force was no longer needed. They stayed off the coast of Guatemala for a further six weeks but were never called on to fight. Chuck did not forget his feelings that first night, but as the sense of danger faded and life assumed a more normal routine, he became less aware of them and of God.

Back in the USA Chuck was ready for new challenges. He resigned and became a member of the Reserves. Then he started on the next stage of his career – law and politics.

CHAPTER TWO

Young Kingmaker

The day he graduated from college in 1953 was important for Chuck in more ways than one. Not only was it the end of his college career, it was also his wedding day. He married Nancy Billings, a young woman from Boston, and their first child, a boy called Wendell, was born in 1954. They had their second son, Christian, in 1956 and, finally, a daughter, Emily, in 1958.

After Chuck left the Marines in 1955 he and Nancy moved to Washington DC. Nancy, a devoted mother, spent her time bringing up the children. Chuck meanwhile began a job as Assistant to the Assistant Secretary of the Navy, a very good position for someone who was only twenty-three. Like his father before him, Chuck decided to study law at night school and enrolled at the George Washington University.

Chuck's job at the Navy Department did not last very long. During his first year in Washington he met Leverett Saltonstall, the Republican senior Senator from Massachusetts. Chuck's father was an ardent Republican and Chuck had grown up to believe fervently in the Republican cause. He had found politics fascinating ever since, at the age of seventeen, he had been a volunteer worker on a campaign for Massachusetts Governor Bradford.

Bradford had lost the campaign but Chuck was firmly hooked. Saltonstall was impressed by the young Chuck Colson and offered him a job on his staff as Executive Secretary. Chuck did not let him down, and two years later Saltonstall promoted him to Administrative Assistant, the youngest in the US Senate. It was not just Saltonstall who was impressed by Chuck. One former member of Saltonstall's staff later described Chuck as 'one of the three or four most talented human beings I've ever encountered'.

In 1960 the US Presidential elections took place and the task of managing Saltonstall's campaign fell to Chuck. It was not an easy task because Saltonstall had a formidable Democratic opponent in the young mayor of Springfield, Massachusetts, Tom O'Connor. The Democrats were popular, especially since Massachusetts' own John F. Kennedy was the Democratic Presidential candidate, standing against the Republican Richard Nixon. Although Chuck had some political experience it was now that he really cut his political teeth

Massachusetts has a large Irish-American population, and they, Chuck believed, could swing the election either way. The opinion polls in the early autumn of 1960 showed that Saltonstall and O'Connor were level pegging. Chuck believed that his man could do better so he devised a plan. He contacted a number of important Irish-American Democrats and asked them to agree to sign a letter supporting Kennedy as President and Saltonstall as Senator. Then he arranged for this letter to be posted to every family in the telephone directory whose name sounded Irish. On the face of it there seemed little wrong with this. Although Kennedy was a Democrat and Saltonstall a Republican, they had often worked together on local issues. But Chuck was not being entirely honest. Saltonstall supported Nixon publicly and had no idea about the letter.

To send the letter to the 300,000 or so Irish-sounding names found in the telephone directory would be quite a feat. Chuck hired several rooms in a downtown Boston hotel and changed the locks on the doors. Then he gathered together two dozen devoted volunteers and asked them to address and stuff thousands of envelopes. Exhausted but inspired, they saw it through and the letters went out. Saltonstall was re-elected by 300,000 votes.

Chuck was elated. It was a first real taste of what he later described as his desire to be a 'political kingmaker'. Saltonstall was, of course, delighted too, though he might well have felt it was a hollow victory if he had known about the Irish letter. He asked Chuck to stay on as his Administrative Assistant, but, as usual, Chuck was ready for a new challenge – a law practice.

By now Chuck had a reputation as a very bright, young lawyer, and it was not surprising when several Boston law firms offered him posts. Chuck turned them down. Instead, he joined up with a friend and fellow lawyer Charlie Morin and they sunk Chuck's savings – $5,000 – into setting up a law firm. They decided to go for a two-pronged approach and opened an office in both Boston and Washington DC.

Chuck and Charlie were aware of prejudice against them when they started up. Chuck, after all, was not from Harvard, and Charlie, although Harvard-educated, was a Catholic with an Irish-Canadian background. They were both perceived as outsiders, and they soon compounded this apparent drawback by employing another lawyer, Joe Mitchell. Joe was very highly qualified but had had problems finding work. The reason was that he was black. Despite the opinions of the legal establishment, Chuck and Charlie's firm began to thrive. Joe proved such an asset that several other law firms tried to poach him from them, no longer worried that a black lawyer would harm their business.

There were, however, worrying times when the bills outstripped the cheques. One snowy night in December 1962 Charlie and Chuck pored over the firm's accounts. They owed a lot of money and business was slowing down. The future looked bleak and it seemed that they might have bitten off more than they could chew. The next day Chuck flew home to Washington. As he flew he found his thoughts wandering back to his time in the Marines when he had served under General Puller. Once, on a training exercise in the Caribbean, Puller had ordered Chuck and his men to climb a seemingly unscaleable cliff. It had appeared to be impossible, but the men had managed it. The incident had made a deep impression upon Chuck. The principle was the same now, he realized: the firm could succeed if they put everything they had into it.

There, on the plane, he drafted a long letter to Charlie Morin, listing what they should do and the work they would be able to find. Chuck was right. Thanks to their hard work and total dedication, every bit of new business he said they would get came their way. A lawyer who knew Chuck well in those days said: 'If I was about to be strung up for my life, I'd hire Chuck to represent me. My hangman would get hung, and I'd be left standing there.'

Sadly, Chuck did not have the time, nor perhaps the inclination, to put the same amount of effort into his home life. Over the years, Nancy and he began to grow apart and eventually they separated. Their divorce came through in January 1964. This was Chuck's first failure, though at the time he would be the last to admit it as such. Chuck believed in himself too much to accept failure.

Happiness, however, was not far away. Later that year Chuck married for a second time. His new wife was Patty Hughes, who worked as a secretary for the government on Washington's Capitol Hill. Patty was a Catholic and an outgoing woman who shared Chuck's enthusiasm for politics. She was to be the linchpin in his life over the years ahead.

CHAPTER THREE

Life at the Top

Richard Nixon was one of the most influential men in Chuck's life. Born in California in 1913, Nixon grew up in a lower-middle-class, Quaker family who originally came from Ireland. He studied law but spent 1942-46 serving in the US Navy.

Nixon began his political career as soon as he left the Navy. In 1946 he was elected to the House of Representatives, one of the US Government's two elected houses. He soon made himself a formidable reputation as an outspoken and brilliant Republican politician and became Vice-President under President Dwight Eisenhower. In 1960, when Chuck was working for Saltonstall, Nixon was ready to stand for President himself. His opponent was John F. Kennedy. Kennedy just beat Nixon, with a tiny majority, and became the youngest-ever and the first Catholic to be elected President. Three years later, on 22 November 1963, Kennedy was gunned down in Dallas, Texas, in one of the most infamous assassinations ever.

Chuck was very impressed with Nixon. They first met when Nixon was Vice-President and Chuck followed Nixon's career through to 1968 when Nixon stood for President again. That year Chuck took four months off work to help Nixon's campaign, telling his partners at work, 'The country needs Nixon right now.' Nixon was what the country got. He was elected with a small majority and Chuck was rewarded for the part he played in the election. One day, late in 1969, Chuck's telephone rang. It was the White House; the President wanted to see him.

As Chuck was guided through the corridors of the White House his heart beat fast and so loudly that he thought that everyone he passed must have heard it. His destination was the Oval Office, the heart of the White House, where so many decisions had been made which altered the course of history in the twentieth century.

Chuck stepped into the office. Light streamed in through the windows, which stretched from the floor to the ceiling, and reflected off the curved white walls. The light was very slightly green which, Chuck discovered later, was because of the bullet-proof glass in the windows. Spread out on the floor in front of him was a vast, deep blue rug emblazoned with a ring of gold stars and a gold eagle in the middle, representing the President's Seal of Office. High above on the ceiling Chuck caught sight of another replica of the Seal, this time in white plaster. Across the room, behind a mahogany desk so large that several people could have sat comfortably around it, and flanked by tall flags, was President Nixon, believed by many to be the most important man in the world. Chuck stood tall and proud before the President. Just thirty-eight years old, he felt as if his life was fulfilled.

Nixon offered Chuck the post of Special Counsel to the President, a legal and political adviser. Chuck was soon installed in his own office in the Executive Office Building, a Victorian construction with turrets. Most of the White House staff had offices there, and from Chuck's room he could look out at the White House and the trees on the sunny south lawn. It was a lovely view, but Chuck did not have much time to gaze out at it. He threw himself into his work with the same enthusiasm that he had tackled everything in his life and soon gained the reputation of a man who got things done, regardless of any obstacles.

In fact, Chuck became fairly ruthlesss. If he had to make a decision without consulting everyone involved, it rarely worried him. He was also happy to leak stories to the press, sometimes damaging or enhancing reputations. According to author Fawn Brodie, in her book *Richard Nixon: The Shaping of His Character*, Chuck had even tried to leak a story to *Life* magazine implicating John Kennedy in the assassination of the deposed President Diem of South Vietnam. Chuck, however, was not alone in leaking stories to the press, and sometimes was at the receiving end of similar treatment.

Chuck took up his post as the Vietnam War, America's longest war, was dragging itself slowly towards an end. Indirectly, Vietnam was to cause Chuck a lot of trouble.

Since the end of the Second World War, the USA had seen its international role as defending the non-communist world against communist encroachments. Thus the period known as the Cold War began, and the main US opponent was the Soviet Union. Vietnam was part of this Cold War policy.

Vietnam was divided into two separate countries – North and South. The US backed the South, while the North was communist and was supported by the Soviet Union and China.

North Vietnam wanted the country united – with the South under the control of the Government in the Northern capital, Hanoi – and began to take steps to bring this about. Soon the American Government was watching with alarm as the Viet Cong, a communist guerrilla force, attacked and killed hundreds of South Vietnamese. Fighting alongside the Viet Cong was the official North Vietnamese army. When it seemed that South Vietnam would be unable to defend itself against the North, the Americans sent in military advisers to help the South. By the middle of 1962 President Kennedy had authorized 5,000 American troops to be sent to South Vietnam. Kennedy did not live to see the results of his decision – the USA involved in a full-scale war which killed 58,000 American soldiers and left thousands more with mental and physical scars.

The Vietnam War was massively unpopular among some sectors of American society, particularly the young and students. Perhaps as many as a quarter of a million young men refused to register for the military draft and 50,000 more left the country to avoid being called up. There were regular marches and demonstrations across the country protesting against the war and against the Government. The Democratic Party wanted an early withdrawal of American troops from Vietnam and among those leading the protests against the war was the Democratic Senator Harold Hughes. He and Chuck disliked each other because of their opposing views.

Although, like most Americans, Chuck did not like what was happening in Vietnam and wanted the war to end, he did not support the anti-war protesters. He believed that the USA had to continue defending the South Vietnamese until they could reach a peace agreement with the North. He therefore opposed the anti-war movement and did what he could to discredit it. On one occasion, for instance, he asked John Dean, Counsel to the President, to investigate the military records of some soldiers who had fought in Vietnam but who were now speaking out against the war. He hoped that Dean would discover details about possible misconduct in the Army which could be used against them. Dean, however, found nothing.

One evening, however, Chuck's confidence in what the American Government was doing in Vietnam was rather shaken. Nixon had already begun withdrawing American troops from Vietnam in 1969, but on 30 April 1970 he had authorized troops to enter neighbouring Cambodia to attack North Vietnamese and Viet Cong forces who were hiding there. Chuck had supported him in this, but the decision was greeted with shock and dismay throughout the USA. Protests flooded in from everyone, from senators to church leaders to students, and there were demonstrations at universities across the country. One of them ended in tragedy.

Chuck was having a late meal in the White House

that evening. As he sat down to eat in the oak-panelled dining room he glanced up at the large television in the corner. What he saw stunned and horrified him and his fellow diners. A news report was showing scenes of a student demonstration at Kent State University in Ohio. The demonstration had got out of hand and the National Guard had opened fire on the students. Suddenly Chuck saw a young woman screaming as she knelt beside the body of a dead friend. The picture froze him. Then a man, Mr Krause, appeared on the television, his face distorted by his sobs. His nineteen-year-old daughter Allison was dead and he cried out, 'The President is to blame!'

Chuck was indignant. How dare that man say something like that. Of course the President was not to blame. Then he had another thought. Supposing his own daughter Emily had been at the demonstration and she had been shot dead? How would he have felt? He, too, would probably have blamed Nixon. And if Nixon were to blame, he too was guilty because he had supported the President in his decision to attack Cambodia. 'For one awful instant,' wrote Chuck in his autobiography, *Born Again*, 'I felt that Mr Krause was right in that room, that his tear-filled eyes were looking straight into mine, and I felt unclean.'[1]

The next day Nixon promised to withdraw all the troops from Cambodia within the next three to seven weeks, but not everybody was satisfied. For days afterwards there were strikes and demonstrations across university campuses, and more deaths as the police fired on students. Then on

Saturday 9 May more than 150,000 demonstrators – mainly students – arrived in Washington and set off for the White House.

The Government took demonstrations very seriously, to the extent of having a set of rooms which acted as a 'command post' deep in the White House from where the President could watch what was going on outside. The 'command post' had supplies, beds, three television sets, radio equipment, telephones, and even a desk with flags on it for the President to sit at. On the morning of 9 May there was a battalion of soldiers in the Executive Office Building, wearing full battle dress, complete with camouflaged helmets. It reminded Chuck of the times he had seen soldiers protecting the President's palace in Central American countries, and he thought anxiously, 'This should not be happening here in the US.'

Chuck spent the day of the demonstration in the White House, watching as crowds of angry people thronged the streets demanding the withdrawal of American forces from both Cambodia and Vietnam. Some of them carried coffins draped in black crêpe paper and marked with the words 'Viet Dead'. Others wore gas masks and surgical masks and carried sticks and poles; they shouted abuse at Nixon and the White House. As the demonstrators approached the White House the police charged into the crowd, swinging clubs and wearing gas masks to protect themselves from the acrid tear gas which was being fired at the protesters. The tear gas and the police proved too much for the crowd and the emergency was soon over.

The memory, however, remained. Even after Nixon had regained some of his popularity the Government was wary. Throughout the White House there was a sense of paranoia, a feeling that the Government was under siege.

One of the Government's biggest perceived enemies was the media. Chuck was to have many clashes with the newspapers and television. As articles and programmes continued to oppose the Vietnam War, he became more and more suspicious of and angry with them. In fact, he described himself as 'a flag-waving, anti-press, anti-liberal Nixon fanatic'.[2] The *New York Times* was viewed as a particular enemy and White House staff were forbidden to talk to any reporter from that paper. However it was the *Washington Post* that was to prove the most damaging.

The Government's feelings of paranoia were not helped by the way that stories were leaked to the press. There were often reports in the newspapers of Government strategy and plans that the Government wanted to be kept secret, at least for the time being. So worried did Nixon and his staff become that in July 1971 they set up a Special Investigations Unit, known as the Plumbers' Unit, to stop the leaks. The Unit's first and most important task was to stop the press finding out the full details of the Pentagon Papers.

The Pentagon Papers were top secret. They were reports of the USA's early involvement in Vietnam and showed that the war had been poorly planned and that Congress and the public had not been told the whole truth about it. The man telling the press about this was Daniel Ellsberg. He had originally been involved in drawing up the plans for the Vietnam War and now wanted to expose what had been said.

If the press found out the details of the Pentagon Papers it would be very embarrassing and damaging for the Government, and could also endanger what the US forces were doing in Vietnam. At the same time, Nixon was involved in some very delicate, secret negotiations with China, designed to open up relations between the US and China. Revelations from the Pentagon Papers could seriously damage these negotiations.

Ellsberg was to be tried in court on a charge of stealing Government documents, but the press called him a champion of the public's right to know what was going on. Chuck, however, was horrified by what Ellsberg was doing. Some people thought Ellsberg was a communist and Nixon believed that he was a traitor. He called Chuck in to a meeting to discuss what they should do. Nixon was furious, pacing the room and venting his anger about Ellsberg. Nixon looked at Chuck and saw in him a man capable of stopping the 'traitor', so he gave him the order that was to cause Chuck plenty of trouble in the future – to discredit Ellsberg in the public's eyes.

Chuck scarcely needed to be told. While the Government was trying to get the courts to forbid publication of the Pentagon Papers, he would make sure that the press were fed information showing that Ellsberg was nothing more than a villain. It did not matter to him that some of the information he passed on was confidential, nor that it might have an effect on the impartiality of Ellsberg's forthcoming trial. Such considerations seemed unimportant compared with the need to protect the Government's policy on such life-and-death issues as the Vietnam War. John Dean, in his book *Blind Ambition*, even reports a time when one of his distressed staff told him that Chuck wanted him to firebomb a building in order to find some documents belonging to an Ellsberg associate. Fortunately, this never happened.

It was around this time that Chuck started to be known as Nixon's 'hatchet man', a title first given him by the *Wall Street Journal* in October 1971. The newspaper printed the headline 'Nixon Hatchet Man: Call it what you will, Chuck Colson handles President's dirty work'. It quoted Chuck's comment to a White House visitor: 'I would do anything Richard Nixon asks me to do – period.'

There were, however, men who were prepared to do far dirtier work to help the President – Howard Hunt and Gordon Liddy. Like Chuck, Hunt was a graduate of Brown University, though he graduated several years before Chuck. They had met at the Brown University Club in Washington back in 1966, and Chuck recommended Hunt to help in the investigation of Ellsberg. Hunt, a novelist, used to work with the Central Intelligence Agency (CIA) and was very tough and loyal to the Government. Gordon Liddy was equally tough and loyal and had worked for the Federal Bureau of Investigation (FBI). Unfortunately Liddy and Hunt were thoroughly unscrupulous and were to cause Nixon,

Chuck and many others a great deal of trouble in the following years.

At one time Ellsberg had been seeing a psychiatrist in Los Angeles called Dr Fielding. Liddy and Hunt thought that this might give them a perfect opportunity to suggest that Ellsberg was not to be trusted. They knew, of course, that Dr Fielding would not give them his former patient's records, so they decided to break in to his offices and steal them. They took with them a number of Cuban men who, the following year, were caught breaking into some more famous offices – the Democratic Party's National Committee offices in a building called Watergate.

Notes

1 Charles Colson, *Born Again*, London, Hodder & Stoughton, 1979.
2 William Safire, *Before the Fall*, New York, Doubleday & Company, 1975.

CHAPTER FOUR

Tarnished Victory

Chuck may not have shown himself to be a great judge of character in recommending Hunt for appointment, but he still knew how to help his party win elections. The following year, 1972, was election year and President Nixon was going all out for re-election. Beside him was Chuck, his 'hatchet man'.

Chuck and Nixon agreed that one way to win votes was to go for a tough stand on law and order. It was more than just an election ploy however – it was something Chuck fervently believed in. Crime was – and still is – a growing problem in the USA and Chuck believed in increasing the powers of the police and in imposing long prison sentences as a way of curbing it. He also believed that the public agreed with him; that good, old-fashioned Middle Americans were tired of what they dubbed 'the era of permissiveness' that modern society had entered. Throughout the election campaign he and other Republicans spoke of the need to be tough – on drugs, on abortion, on young men who had refused to join the forces to fight in the Vietnam War (known as 'draft dodgers'), and on all criminals. They also accused their opponents, the Democrats, of being 'soft' on these issues. The Republicans were the ones who supported the law, honesty and decency.

The Republican stand seemed to work and Nixon inched ahead in the opinion polls. But it was foreign policy that really made the difference. Early in 1972 Nixon became convinced that secret negotiations with the North Vietnamese – that had been going on for the past two and a half years, aimed at ending the Vietnam War – were not working. Instead he made a new and public peace offer and announced that he would more than halve the number of American troops in Vietnam (to 69,000) and withdraw them all within six months of a peace settlement. Chuck had known about the negotiations, but they were a well-kept secret. The public were very surprised and impressed. They saw the President as a statesman who had been patiently negotiating for the past few years to win the best settlement for South Vietnam and for America.

Unfortunately the North Vietnamese took it as a sign that America was weakening and in March 1972 launched a new invasion of the South. They did not think South Vietnam would last long. Nixon was faced with one of the most difficult decisions he had ever had to make. Should he do nothing and perhaps watch South Vietnam capitulate? This would be a humiliation for the USA. Nixon knew that the country could not afford such a humiliation because he was about to enter into negotiations with the Soviet Union in Moscow, who had been supporting the North Vietnamese. On the other hand, reversing his decision to withdraw American troops from Vietnam could also endanger his negotiations and might make the war last even longer, with even more lives lost.

In the end Nixon decided to bomb the North Vietnamese, even though his advisers told him this could make him so unpopular that he might lose the election. Nixon, however, believed that this was something he had to do, regardless of the effects on his own career, and Chuck admired this decision. He believed that the President was putting the needs of the country before his own ambitions.

The tough policy paid off. The North Vietnamese action was curbed, the Moscow conference went ahead and, despite criticism from the media and from the anti-war lobby, large sections of the public supported Nixon. All through the year the Government's popularity grew and grew. In February 1972, just before the new Vietnam crisis, Nixon had made a historic trip to China, opening the channels for future co-operation between the two. The visit was televised live and millions of Americans watched. The President's popularity rose in leaps and bounds. In August, with just three months to go before the election, Nixon was twenty points ahead of his Democratic rival Senator George McGovern in the opinion polls. There could be little doubt that he would be re-elected.

There was just one small, dark cloud on the horizon. One Saturday morning, 17 June 1972, while Chuck was driving through Washington, he had heard a short news bulletin on the car radio about a break-in at the Democratic National Committee offices in the prestigious Watergate complex on the banks of the Potomac river. He did not give much thought to the news item at the time, but later that day John Erhlichman, the President's adviser on

Domestic Affairs, telephoned him.

He asked what had happened to Howard Hunt, the man Chuck had recommended to work on the Ellsberg case. Chuck was surprised: he had not seen Hunt for a long time. He was sure Hunt was not even working for the White House any more and told Ehrlichman so. Ehrlichman, however, sounded as if something was seriously wrong. Then he broke the news – one of the burglars at the Democratic Headquarters had a cheque in his pocket with Hunt's name on it. Chuck was stunned. This simply was not possible. Hunt would not be so stupid as to be involved in a break-in at the Democratic offices. But if he was, people might link him with Chuck. After all, Chuck had recommended him.

Ehrlichman rang off and Chuck went to sit by his swimming pool. He had been planning to take a swim but now the water did not look so inviting. Instead he sat and thought anxiously about what had happened and when he had last seen Hunt. He thought it was in February, when Hunt and Liddy had been working on a plan to improve the White House's knowledge of who was behind demonstrations and the anti-war movement.

The next day Chuck rushed to read the newspaper. The *Washington Post* had printed a story about the break-in under the headline 'Five held in plot to bug Democratic Party office'. Apparently the burglars were carrying recording equipment and were planning to bug the offices. Much to Chuck's relief there was no mention of Hunt, but the relief was short-lived. By Monday the press had got hold of Hunt's name and were ringing Chuck about it.

On Tuesday one of the papers, the *Star*, had a front-page headline which announced 'Colson aide – Barker tied'. Barker was one of the men arrested for the break-in; the aide was Howard Hunt.

The White House staff, including Chuck, were thrown into a panic after the Watergate break-in. It would be very damaging to the Government if it were revealed that any of the President's staff were involved in the incident, not to mention the criminal charges that could be brought against them. But the public seemed unaware of what was going on, and Nixon's popularity was unharmed. Then, in September, the five burglars were indicted (formally charged) for their actions, along with Howard Hunt and Gordon Liddy. The US Justice Department said, 'We have absolutely no evidence to indicate that any others should be charged.' The heat, it seemed, was off the White House.

Election day, 7 November, arrived and American citizens went to the polling booths. By the evening it was clear that Nixon would be re-elected. Chuck, his wife Patty and his eldest son Wendell, then just eighteen years old, attended a Republican victory party at the Shoreham Hotel in Washington. As they gathered in the hotel ballroom to watch the results coming in, Chuck knew he should feel elated and proud. Nixon was going to break all the previous records and it had been Chuck's hard work that had helped him to do so. Instead, Chuck felt worn out and, try as he might, he simply could not feel as excited as he had expected.

He looked around the room. It seemed that everyone else felt like he did. The faces he saw seemed to look disappointed. Perhaps they were simply worn out too. Some of them were no doubt wondering where the President was, believing rightly, Chuck felt, that the President should have been there to greet his loyal supporters who had done so much to help re-elect him. 'Come to think of it,' said Chuck to himself as he continued looking around, 'I seem to be the only senior member of the White House staff here.'

As he continued to wander around the room, looking at the glum faces and hearing false laughter and shrill voices, he received a summons to the White House. It came as a relief, though he felt that Wendell might be a little disappointed to have to leave too. The chance to ride in a limousine and visit the Executive Office Building were some compensation and Chuck left Patty and Wendell in his own office while he slipped in for a few minutes to see Nixon. Unfortunately for Patty and Wendell the few minutes turned into a few tedious hours while Chuck sat with Nixon as he tried to write a telegram to Senator McGovern, the man he had beaten in the elections.

Bob Haldeman, the White House's Chief of Staff, was also in the office, reading through the election results as they came in. Like Chuck, Haldeman seemed glum as he added up the figures to give an accurate picture of how well Nixon had done. 'From the look of him you'd think we'd lost, not won by the greatest margin ever,' thought Chuck as he sipped a scotch and soda. 'If someone outside could see us now, what would they think?' he wondered. There was the President, at his hour of victory, struggling to write something magnanimous to his opponent; sitting near him at a small table was the Chief of Staff, looking angry and occasionally shouting down the telephone at his assistant; and there was Chuck, the man who had done so much to bring about this victory, slumped down in a stupor, feeling numb. 'If this is victory, what would we be like in defeat?' he wondered.

That night Chuck had only a few hours' sleep. He had planned to have a lie-in the next morning, but the harsh ringing noise of the special White House telephone woke him at eight o'clock. It was an immediate summons to the White House. Chuck groaned. It was unfair to expect him to work at this time of the morning after just four hours' sleep. However, when the President called, Chuck knew he had to obey.

He joined the other senior White House staff in the Roosevelt Room, just across a narrow corridor from the Oval Office. Everyone looked drawn and tired, which was not surprising after all the hard work in the preceding weeks and the hard drinking that had gone on at the victory party the night before. However they all leapt up enthusiastically when Nixon walked in.

Nixon smiled and motioned them to sit down. Then he began to speak, thanking the staff for their work. However, few people were prepared for what came next. Nixon continued:

I was reading Disraeli the other night, and Disraeli spoke of how his administration of the British Government lost its spark after being re-elected. The campaign took too much out of them, he said. They became a 'burned-out volcano', fresh out of ideas and energy. Well, I thought about that, and I pledged to myself that no such thing will happen to this Second Administration. I am not a burned-out volcano, and the Second Administration will not become one either. We are going to inject new vigour and new energy into the Government. We have no choice but to do that. Our opportunity is too great. Our responsibility is too great. The American people have just spoken and given us a tremendous mandate, a vote of confidence and hope. We can build a generation of peace, with prosperity, in America, and we are going to get on with the job. Now Bob [Haldeman] is going to talk to you about some of the specifics. I want to thank you all again.[1]

The staff applauded, a little puzzled. However it soon became clear what Nixon had meant. The 'specifics' were that all the staff were to hand in their resignations. There would, of course, Haldeman said, be opportunities for new jobs, and staff should say what jobs they would like and how they thought they were qualified for them. This was some comfort, but Chuck and the others were stunned. Didn't they deserve better treatment than this after the months of hard work? Some of them had worked for Nixon for years. Chuck had already decided that he would leave the White House and return to his law practice with Charlie Morin, but he did not relish the thought of telling his own staff to resign and then of finding them other jobs. He had not even allowed them to take holidays that year.

Later, Nixon told Chuck that he wanted him to stay on. It was flattering to be asked, but Chuck wanted to leave. He was tired and he could not shake off the feeling that something was badly wrong.

Note

1 John Dean, *Blind Ambition*, New York, Simon and Schuster, 1976.

CHAPTER FIVE

A Brief History of Watergate

Watergate was the most serious scandal to affect modern American politics. It started with the arrest of five burglars and ended with the resignation and threatened impeachment of the President of the United States of America – Richard Nixon.

The scandal takes its name from the Watergate complex overlooking the Potomac river. Inside this rather menacing looking block is a hotel, some offices and a number of residential apartments. Among the residents in 1972 were several very prominent Republican figures including John Mitchell, former Attorney General and, in June 1972, Director of the Committee to Re-elect the President; Senator Robert Dole, the Republican National Chairman; and Rosemary Woods, President Nixon's secretary. The Watergate building was, in fact, seen by many as a symbol of Richard Nixon's rule in Washington, so much so that in 1970 a group of 1,000 anti-Nixon demonstrators had tried to attack the building, yelling 'Fascists', 'Pigs', and 'Sieg Heil'. Watergate was, therefore, something of a strange place for the Democratic Party to have its National Committee Head-quarters, but the Democrats took up the whole of the sixth floor.

In the early hours of Saturday 17 June 1972, three

plain-clothed police officers burst into the Democrat offices and arrested five men found hiding behind a desk. They were unusual-looking burglars: they were dressed in business suits and carried films, a short-wave receiver for picking up police calls, a walkie-talkie, tiny tear gas guns and sophisticated bugging equipment. They all wore thin surgical gloves and had about $2,300 on them, most of it in $100 notes. They had their own rooms booked in the hotel and had eaten lobster in the restaurant on Friday evening. They were clearly not ordinary burglars.

It soon emerged that one of the burglars, James McCord, had worked for the CIA. The other men were Cubans from Miami where they were also said to have connections with the CIA. This was suspicious enough, but what first linked them with the White House was that one of the men had some papers and a cheque with Howard Hunt's name on it. Immediate suspicion fell upon the White House and the Committee to Re-elect the President (CRP).

Recognizing the danger that this suspicion posed to the Government and for Nixon's chances of being re-elected in the November 1972 elections, the White House immediately began a cover-up operation. White House officials announced that the burglars were acting alone. On 22 June President Nixon himself made a public statement: 'The White House has no involvement whatever in this particular incident.' Many people, including two reporters from the *Washington Post*, Carl Bernstein and Bob Woodward, did not believe him. Meanwhile, further bugging equipment had been found at the

Democratic offices. The burglars had obviously been there before.

Over in the White House there was frantic activity. Howard Hunt was told to go abroad, and sensitive papers in his and other White House safes were destroyed. Among the information believed to have been destroyed was actual proof of wire-tapping. John Mitchell, Director of the CRP, resigned for 'personal reasons'. Gordon Liddy, who had hired McCord to do the break-in (Hunt provided the other four men), even offered to let himself be killed in an apparently random street shooting if that would help protect the White House from further investigation. 'You just let me know when and where, and I'll be there,' he told a horrified John Dean, Counsel to Nixon.

The White House put pressure on the FBI to limit its investigation to the five burglars and to Hunt and Liddy. The White House and the CRP paid for their defence and also paid the seven men 'hush money', mainly from funds collected by the CRP. Newspaper reporters, including Bernstein and Woodward, found out about this money and their investigations led to the discovery that the CRP had been paying people to sabotage Democrat election chances throughout the USA by using underhand tricks. They also discovered that White House officials had approved other illegal activities such as the break-in at Daniel Ellsberg's psychiatrist's office.

To keep the public at bay, in August 1972 President Nixon announced that his Counsel, John Dean had carried out an internal investigation, and that, 'I can say categorically that his investigation indicates that no one in the White House staff, no one in this Administration, presently employed, was involved in this very bizarre incident.' John Dean was as surprised as anyone at this announcement: he had made no such investigation. If the President was not lying before, he certainly was now. He was also well aware of the cover-up.

In January 1973 the five Watergate burglars, Howard Hunt and Gordon Liddy were tried for their involvement in the break-in and bugging. They were all found guilty, but Judge John Sirica who sentenced them stressed that he believed that there were others involved and urged that the investigation continue.

The following month the US Senate appointed a committee under Senator Sam Ervin to begin its own investigation. This put a great deal of pressure on the White House, calling staff before the committee and questioning them in front of television cameras. The nation watched as evidence accumulated against not just senior White House officials, but against the President himself.

In an effort to protect both Richard Nixon and the Office of President itself, several senior members of the Administration resigned. Bob Haldeman, White House Chief of Staff; John Ehrlichman, Assistant to the President for Domestic Affairs; and Richard Kleindienst, the Attorney General who had directed the prosecution of the burglars, all resigned at the end of April 1973. John Dean, who had worked for Haldeman, was fired. Chuck Colson had already left the White House staff to return to his private law firm.

Dean decided to testify before the committee and his evidence helped to convince many that Richard Nixon had known about Hunt and Liddy's undercover activities and about the Watergate cover-up. Meanwhile, the Ervin Committee also discovered that Nixon had taped all his conversations and meetings.

In May 1973 Nixon appointed Archibald Cox as Special Prosecutor to investigate the cover-up. Cox subpoenaed the tapes of his conversations, but the president refused to relinquish them, claiming 'Executive privilege'. Cox insisted, and by October Nixon had had enough. He asked the Attorney General Elliot Richardson and his Assistant William Ruckelshaus to dismiss Cox. When they refused Nixon fired them and appointed an Acting Attorney General who was willing to fire Cox. There was immediate public uproar, so less than two weeks later Nixon, who had wanted to abolish the post of Special Prosecutor altogether, appointed Leon Jaworski in Cox's place.

In November 1973 Nixon handed over seven tapes to Jaworski, saying that these were the only ones relevant to the Watergate investigation. They did not reveal any direct link between Nixon and the Watergate scandal, but they did little to improve Nixon's standing with the nation. They showed him to be vindictive, at times vacillating, and certainly profane. One tape had an eighteen-and-a-half-minute gap during which all that could be heard was a two-tone humming noise. The humming erased a discussion between Nixon and Haldeman on 20 June 1972 about the Watergate scandal.

At the same time, the investigation was revealing past corruption in the Administration, gifts to Nixon in return for political favours and the fact that Nixon had not paid his taxes for the years 1969 to 1972. Yet Nixon was not the only one in the Administration who was accused of dubious financial dealings. Vice-President Spiro Agnew was also charged with accepting bribes and failing to pay his income tax. He resigned and was convicted on one charge of tax evasion. This did little to help Nixon's cause. Gerald Ford was appointed as the new Vice-President.

By the end of February 1974 the Watergate prosecutors had obtained guilty pleas from seven men who had worked either for the White House or the CRP or both. Eight corporations and their officers had pleaded guilty to charges of making illegal contributions to the CRP; Dwight Chapin, the President's Deputy Assistant, had been charged with perjury; and Mitchell and Maurice Stans, Finance Chairman of the CRP, were on trial charged with perjury and obstruction of justice.

In March 1974 Mitchell, Haldeman, Ehrlichman, Chuck Colson, and various White House and CRP aides were all indicted by a grand jury with conspiracy to obstruct justice. Nixon was named as an unindicted co-conspirator. A week later Ehrlichman, Chuck, Liddy and three Cuban-Americans – including two of the original Watergate burglars – were indicted for a conspiracy to burgle the offices of Daniel Ellsberg's psychiatrist, Dr Fielding.

There had never been anything like this in American political history. The Administration was in tatters and Nixon had become an isolated, unpopular figure. The courts trying the Watergate case ordered Nixon to give them more tapes, but instead he produced edited transcripts which suggested he was involved in the cover-up, although they did not prove it.

In July the House Judiciary Committee voted that three Articles of Impeach-ment be brought against President Nixon. He was accused of obstructing justice, abusing Presidential power and refusing to answer Congressional subpoenas. On 5 August Nixon released transcripts of three more tapes which clearly showed that he had ordered the FBI to stop the investigation of the Watergate break-in. Nixon's advisers persuaded him to resign and three days later, on 8 August 1974, he did so.

Gerald Ford, who had been Vice-President for less than a year, took over the Presidency. On 8 September he granted Nixon a pardon for any crimes he might have committed. Nixon's staff did not escape so lightly. A number of them were found guilty for their role in the scandal and several of them, including Chuck Colson, went to prison. Ironically, the real reasons for bugging the Watergate offices were never made clear.

CHAPTER SIX

Empty Life

Chuck left the White House soon after the election to return to his law practice which was now called Colson and Shapiro. Charlie Morin was still there and had been joined by other partners including Dave Shapiro, a man who was to become very important to Chuck over the next year. The firm was glad to have Chuck back, so much so that, as a 'welcome back' present, they bought Chuck an expensive limousine and hired a chauffeur. Chuck was touched by their generosity and their welcome. 'It's good to be back,' he thought. He also hoped that being back would give him new challenges and incentives. 'It's what I need,' he told himself. 'This should help me shake off my lethargy.'

Ever since the election Chuck had felt tired. He seemed to have lost some of his enthusiasm for life and for his work. He tried to throw himself back into his law practice, but he could not summon up the excitement he used to feel. Even when important law cases came his way, which would bring in large sums of money, he almost felt indifferent and had to struggle to hide these feelings from his clients and from his fellow lawyers. He could not escape the feeling that something was badly wrong.

At first Chuck thought that he might be ill, but he seemed healthy enough. Then he decided that it must be his age. He knew that lots of men around his age went through a crisis time, when they queried where they were going with their careers and relationships, when they doubted their own worth and their plans for the future. But Chuck and his wife Patty had a happy marriage and Chuck had a very fulfilling career. Eventually Chuck decided that what he was feeling was simply a reaction from the tense and busy years spent at the White House. In time, he believed, he would settle down and life would get back to normal. In the meantime he wanted to concentrate on earning some money. As a lawyer earning a salary which went into six figures Chuck had become used to a very comfortable lifestyle. Four years of working at the White House on a government salary had made a large dent in his bank balance and Chuck wanted to improve his financial position.

One of Chuck's clients was the electronics manufacturer the Raytheon Company, based in Chuck's old hometown Boston. Raytheon was a huge success and employed more people in New England than any other company. Its President was Tom Phillips, a tough, aggressive businessman whom Chuck admired for his ability and drive. Chuck flew to Boston in March 1973 to see the company's Executive Vice-President, his old friend Brainerd Holmes, and to become the company's legal adviser, a position he had held several years before. Chuck enjoyed meeting Brainerd again and was pleased when he received a message that Tom Phillips wanted to see him too.

Just as he was leaving to call in on Tom, Brainerd,

clearly a little awkward, told Chuck that he might find Tom a little different on account of a 'religious experience'. Chuck was surprised and puzzled. He could not imagine a religious Tom Phillips. He entered Tom's office, curious to know what the difference would be. At first he thought Tom was the same. He looked the same – friendly and fit, sitting at his desk without a jacket on in his normal, informal way. But Chuck was soon struck by how relaxed Tom was and how genuinely pleased he seemed to see Chuck. There was a real warmth and gentleness about Tom.

The two men chatted for a while and inevitably the conversation turned to Watergate and Chuck's involvement. Chuck was on the defensive. The press had been accusing him of all kinds of things, and Chuck wanted to point out that he had had nothing to do with the burglary. Before he had said more than a few sentences about it, Tom stopped him, assuring him that he believed him. This, too, was strange. Chuck was becoming used to people – mainly the press – disbelieving him. Tom, however, was taking him at his word.

Eventually, Chuck plucked up the courage to ask Tom about his religious experience, unsure what he would hear in reply. He certainly did not expect the answer he received: 'I have accepted Jesus Christ. I have committed my life to him and it has been the most marvellous experience of my whole life.'

Chuck was stunned. What on earth did Tom mean? Jesus Christ lived – and died – 2,000 years ago. And why would anyone 'commit their life' to him? All this was on the tip of Chuck's tongue, but he could not bring himself to say it. Instead he muttered something about 'discussing it sometime' and was relieved when the topic of conversation changed.

Just as Chuck was leaving, Tom said, 'I would like to tell you the whole story some day, Chuck. I had gotten to the point where I didn't think my life was worth anything. Now everything is changed – attitude, values, the whole bit.' Chuck was even more astonished. Tom Phillips had everything anybody could want, or so it seemed. Wealth, success, a good family and home. He could hardly be described as having an empty life. Nor, for that matter, could Chuck, but what Tom had said had struck home. Chuck's own life felt empty, and he had no idea why.

When Chuck returned to Washington the Watergate situation was hotting up. The press accused Chuck of being behind the break-in at the Watergate offices, and however much he denied it, they did not believe him. The news reporters' attitude was a far cry from the one Chuck had encountered in Tom Phillips. Chuck discovered that even his partner and friend Dave Shapiro was not convinced he was innocent.

One evening, after a particularly vicious period of attacks by the press, Dave suggested that Chuck should take a lie-detector test. Chuck was not at all happy with the idea. For a start he did not know how successful such tests were, and, in any case, his nerves were so much on edge that he thought he might appear to be lying when he was really telling the truth. Eventually, however, Dave persuaded

Chuck to visit a man in New York, Richard Arther, who ran a 'scientific detection service'.

As Chuck walked through the New York rain on his way to Arther's office he almost felt like a criminal. He was headed for a rather run-down, old building in the theatre district. Neon lights flashed around him as he passed old cinemas and theatres, and cars splashed water from the gutters on him as he hurried along the soaking streets. He found Arther's building and rode up to the eleventh floor in an ancient, creaking lift. His sense of being a criminal increased as he walked down the long corridor, looking for the correct office. What was he doing here? he wondered. He had hardly slept the night before, his stomach was churning and he was almost shaking with nerves. Worse, it was his tenth wedding anniversary that day. He wanted to be at home with Patty, celebrating, not here in this dreadful building which reminded him of the set of a 1940s detective movie.

Eventually he found Arther's office and, in it, Dave Shapiro and Richard Arther. He called Dave to one side and started to tell him that he could not go through with the test. Dave laughed at first then became serious, promising he would still be his lawyer even if he failed. Suddenly, with a sinking heart, Chuck realized that Dave did not believe him.

To take the test, Chuck had to have wires strapped to his fingers, and a chain around his chest with more wires attached to it. The wires ran into a grey metal box which had small metal arms fixed to it. The arms, in turn, had pencils attached to them, and once the test began, these would draw lines on a moving roll of paper. The arms, Arther explained, would move in response to Chuck's reactions, and, he added, Chuck was not to worry since they were very accurate and reliable. Chuck, however, could not stop worrying. The situation was made worse when Arther told him he should first tell him about all the lies he had ever told so that he could start with a clear conscience. Chuck wanted to leave. The machine, however, seemed to work in the test runs. It picked out when Chuck told a deliberate lie and recorded when he was telling the truth.

Then the real test began. Chuck's heart beat faster and faster when he heard Arther asking whether he had ordered the Watergate break-in. He answered truthfully that he had not, but he was sure that the machine would record that he was telling lies. At the end, Chuck looked down at the long sheet of paper which had rolled down from the machine and on to the floor. It was covered in wavy lines. 'I've failed,' was all Chuck could think. Arther picked up the paper and looked at it carefully. 'Obviously,' thought Chuck, 'he knows I've failed.'

Chuck left the office in a deep depression. The press would have a fine time once they heard about the test, gleefully writing articles about Chuck's involvement in Watergate. The results were meant to be confidential, but Chuck was sure they would find out somehow. He stood in the pouring rain, trying to hail a cab. All he wanted to do was catch the train home to Washington and Patty. What a wedding anniversary it was turning out to be.

Then, just as Chuck was about to clamber into a cab, he heard a loud, deep voice calling behind him, telling him to stop. It was Dave, rushing through the rain without even a jacket on to keep him dry. 'You passed!' he yelled. 'No doubt that you are telling the truth.' Chuck turned to Dave and flung his arms around him. The two men hugged in the pouring rain, oblivious to the people rushing by. The relief was so great that Chuck began to cry.

If Chuck thought life would return to normal, he was mistaken. Although Dave leaked the story of the lie-detector test to the press, it was not long before other stories about Chuck were in the paper too, and most of them blamed him for being involved in Watergate. Chuck learned fast how damaging and intrusive the press can be. There were even camera crews stationed outside his house, and Chuck gave constant interviews.

Sometimes it seemed that the heat was off him. He had, for instance, a lengthy session with the prosecutors who were investigating the Watergate case and they told him that they believed him. Chuck's spirits rose. Then, not long afterwards, Archibald Cox was appointed Special Prosecutor. Immediately Chuck was back in the firing line and Cox wanted to investigate him more. Sometimes Chuck felt almost crushed by what he was going through. All the time, however, he defended President Nixon, on television, radio and in the newspapers. 'The most important person in all this,' thought Chuck, 'is the President. It's my duty to defend him'.

But as Nixon became more vulnerable, and as Vice-President Spiro Agnew began to defend charges of accepting bribes while Governor of

Maryland and of tax evasion (with Chuck's own law firm helping in his defence), so the world that Chuck had believed in for many years began to crumble around him. Chuck felt empty and helpless. He did not know what he was doing with his life. Time and again he thought of Tom Phillips and the certainty and serenity he had exuded. It was time to give him a call.

CHAPTER SEVEN

Alive Again

Chuck was not sure what he would say to Tom Phillips when they met again, but he knew he was looking forward to seeing him. In August Chuck and Patty took a week's holiday in Maine which gave them a chance to stop off at Chuck's parents' in Dover, not far from Boston. Once there, Chuck called Tom on the phone. Tom sounded delighted to hear Chuck's voice. 'Sure, come on over on Sunday evening,' he told Chuck.

Sunday 12 August was a sultry day. The sky was overcast as if it would rain, but the rain refused to come. Instead, the air was heavy and sticky and Chuck was glad of the air-conditioning in his car as he drove towards the Phillips's large, rambling home. He switched off the engine and climbed out on to the drive, wondering which door to the house he should use. He chose the one nearest to him and found that it was the kitchen. Slightly embarrassed, he began to apologize to the tall, friendly woman who opened the door to him. This was Gert, Tom's wife. She and Chuck had never met before but Gert greeted him as if he were an old friend and ushered him into the smart, modern kitchen.

Tom was playing tennis with the children so Gert went to fetch him in. Chuck felt wonderfully at ease. Tom may have been one of the most important businessmen in the State, but his home life seemed comfortingly ordinary. Tom arrived a moment later and shook Chuck warmly by the hand. Then, with glasses of cool ice tea in their hands, he led Chuck through to a porch at the end of the house. 'Sit down,' he said, offering Chuck an outdoor sofa. 'Take your jacket and tie off. It's far too hot to dress like that.' Chuck had dressed smartly in a dark business suit and felt uncomfortably hot.

Tom sat down near him, looked intensely at Chuck and asked him how he was. Chuck knew that this was no mere pleasantry, but that Tom genuinely wanted to know. However, he was not yet prepared to tell Tom exactly how he felt. Instead he changed the subject to Tom himself, and asked him what it was that had so obviously changed his life and made him a happier, more fulfilled person.

So Tom began. He told Chuck about the way he had worked to get where he was at Raytheon. It had been a struggle and he had worked non-stop, determined to get to the top. He was President of the company by the time he was forty. By all accounts he had made it. He had almost everything anyone could want, but he felt empty and incomplete. 'I would go to the office each day and do my job, striving all the time to make the company succeed, but there was a big hole in my life. I began to read the Scriptures, looking for answers. Something made me realize I needed a personal relationship with God.'

Chuck shivered slightly despite the heat. This was making sense. He was not the only one to have these inexplicable feelings of emptiness after all, and perhaps they were not so inexplicable either. He motioned Tom to go on.

One week Tom was in New York on business. He noticed that Billy Graham, the world-famous evangelist, was holding a crusade in the city and decided to go there in the hope of finding something to sooth the emptiness inside and to answer his questions. He listened intently as Billy spoke of Jesus and how men and women could have a personal relationship with him. As he listened Tom realized what was missing in his life, and that night he simply prayed that Jesus would come into his life. When he had done so he felt a definite change – a peace and a certainty that Jesus was with him. From that point on there was no going back.

Chuck sat listening quietly. 'Tom's certainly sincere, there's no doubt of that,' he thought, 'but it can't be that simple. Surely you can't just ask.' He told Tom of his doubts.

Tom assured him all he had to do was ask, though there was one important condition – he genuinely had to want Jesus in his life. 'That's the way it starts,' he said. 'And things then begin to change. Since then I have found a satisfaction and a joy about living that I simply never knew was possible.'

Chuck knew he had a lot of thinking to do before anything similar could happen to him. He took little on trust. His logical, legal mind always needed to probe and ask questions before he could accept any answers. His first stumbling block was that he had always thought of Jesus as a historical figure, not someone alive today.

As their conversation continued, Tom gentiy

pointed out another stumbling block – Chuck's pride. Tom picked up a paperback book and opened it. It was *Mere Christianity* by C. S. Lewis and Tom suggested that Chuck should read it while he was on holiday. But before he handed it to Chuck he read some extracts:

> Pride leads to every other vice: it is the complete anti-God state of mind . . . Nearly all those evils in the world which people put down to greed or selfishness are really far more the result of Pride . . . It is Pride which has been the chief cause of misery in every nation and every family since the world began . . . Pride always means enmity – it is enmity. And not only enmity between man and man but enmity to God . . . As long as you are proud you cannot know God . . . For Pride is a spiritual cancer; it eats up the very possibility of love, or contentment, or even common sense.[1]

Chuck felt his body grow hotter still as he listened to Tom's calm voice. This was just what had happened to him and to many of the other people he had worked with in the White House. Earlier, Tom had pointed out that Watergate and all the other tricks that they had got up to were both unnecessary and wrong. They were not God's way. Now Chuck could see that this was so. He and his colleagues had all been caught up in believing that they were right and that they had to achieve their aims by whatever means were necessary. Just as Lewis had written, there seemed 'no possibility of love, or contentment, or even common sense'.

It was not only in his years at the White House that Chuck had been guilty of the sin of pride. All through his life, he realized, he had struggled to be the best. Although his father had taught him to do everything to the best of his ability, he had gone further than that, at times not caring if he hurt people in his struggle to get to the top. Chuck felt wretched as he thought about the past. Even his first marriage had been partly the result of pride. He had married Nancy Billings partly because of her background. Her parents' social position had helped Chuck on his way as an ambitious young lawyer. Yet how much hurt had he caused Nancy and the children when the marriage failed? Chuck looked at himself and did not like what he saw.

When he had finished reading Tom looked intently at Chuck and said, 'How about it?' Chuck knew what he meant, and for the first time in his life what he was hearing about God made sense. But he was not yet ready to accept Christ into his life. He needed to think some more. He explained to Tom he needed to work through some of his questions first and, more importantly, he needed to know that he was not just turning to God as a prop at a time when he had so many problems in his life. Tom looked a little disappointed but he seemed to understand.

Before Chuck went Tom read him some verses from the Bible, and for the first time Chuck felt the words coming alive to him. 'Trust in the Lord,' read Tom. Chuck had heard those words before in church, for he had attended church when he was younger, but now they meant something to him. He longed to respond and trust, but he still needed to be sure. Then Tom prayed with him, and again Chuck had the sense that this was real. These words were not just pious phrases, said by rote. Tom seemed to be speaking directly to God, asking God to open Chuck's heart. Chuck felt a wave of energy flowing into his body, then a rush of emotion so intense that he had to fight back the tears.

Chuck held his emotions in check until he had said goodbye to Tom and Gert and was in his car. Then the tears began to flow. He tried to stop them but failed, then he thought with a real certainty, 'I must go back and pray with Tom.' He jumped out of the car and was about to walk to the Phillips's door when he saw the lights being turned out. It was too late. Chuck felt terribly alone.

He drove out into the road and set off back to his parents' home, but his tears were flowing so fast that he had to pull over. He sat and sobbed, letting go of his pride, of his fears of appearing weak and inadequate. As he did so he felt a rush of relief and his tears seemed to be cleaning him inside and soothing him. Then he prayed: 'God, I don't know how to find you, but I'm going to try. I'm not much the way I am now, but somehow I want to give myself to you. Take me.'

It was late by the time Chuck returned to Dover, but he and Patty were up early the next morning to drive to Maine. At last they were to have some precious time alone together, and for Chuck it was the ideal opportunity to think about what had happened to him the night before. He knew he felt different after the evening with Tom and he wanted to explore it further. He had not yet accepted Christ into his life, but he suspected he was on the way.

Their destination was Boothbay Harbour, a picturesque, old fishing village four hours' drive from Boston. To their delight they found a small hotel on the edge of a narrow strip of land overlooking the sea. There was one room free for the week, with a massive deck overhanging the sea. Even better, the hotel-keeper did not know what was going on in the Watergate case. His television was broken. It was perfect.

Chuck settled down to read *Mere Christianity* and to think. Ever the lawyer, he wrote the question 'Is there a God?' on a yellow, legal notepad and began to list the points for and against God's existence. One of the problems about believing in God, he decided, was that we cannot see, hear or feel God. Then he stopped. Last night he had felt something or someone, an invisible force, but a force all the same.

The next day Chuck decided to speak to Patty about what he was feeling. Patty was a Roman Catholic but she and Chuck had never really talked about God before. He told her what had happened that night at the Phillips's, though he could not yet bring himself to tell her that he had cried. Patty was surprised at what he said, although she realized that he was sincere and was there to support him.

Chuck struggled on over the next few days, working his way through intellectual problems such as how God could listen to everyone's prayers; and, if God is good, why is the world evil? His legal mind and Lewis's book helped him to find answers which satisfied him – God is not limited by time and space as we are; humans have free will. But he still took a while to come to terms with the statement at the centre of Christianity – Jesus Christ is God. These, Chuck realized, were staggeringly important words. As Lewis said: 'For Christ to have talked as he talked, lived as he lived, died as he died, he was either God or a raving lunatic.'[2] For years, Chuck had believed that Jesus was no more than a prophet and teacher who had been inspired by God, undoubtedly, but nothing more. Yet now, the more he thought about it, the more he realized that this could not have been so, and he could not dismiss Christ as nothing but a lunatic. Could all that had come from Christ's life – the faith of millions, the impact that Christianity has had on the world, the churches – be the result of a lunatic, or simply of a man? Chuck thought not. Gradually it dawned on him: Jesus is God.

The final step was to accept Jesus. Here Chuck still had something of a struggle. He still wondered whether he was grasping at God just because his life was falling apart. People would say that this was the case – 'foxhole religion' he had once called it himself. But Chuck knew he could not avoid making such an important decision just because of what other people might think. He believed in Jesus and therefore he had to decide what to do next.

Early on Friday morning, 17 August 1973, Chuck sat quietly looking out to sea and prayed: 'Lord Jesus, I believe you. I accept you. Please come into my life. I commit it to you.' When he had prayed, a sense of peace and strength enveloped him. All his old fears and tensions seemed to be dissolving and, along with them, the feelings of emptiness and uncertainty that had eaten away at him over the past year. Chuck felt alive again.

Notes

1 C. S. Lewis, *Mere Christianity*, London, Fount, 1952 and subsequently.
2 Ibid.

CHAPTER EIGHT

Early Days

Monday morning 20 August 1973 was much like any other morning, at least outwardly. Chuck's car arrived at 7.30 a.m. just as it always did. His chauffeur was as friendly as usual, though Chuck normally did not pay him much attention. Washington had not changed in the week Chuck and Patty had been on holiday: the traffic was just as heavy and the *Washington Post* was as full of bad news as ever. But that day Chuck saw it all differently. He found himself asking his chauffeur about his family, something he had never thought to do in the past, and there was, he decided, something beautiful about the city in the early morning sun, something fresh and glistening. Chuck recalled Tom Phillips talking about New York on the evening that he had committed his life to Christ: 'I never liked New York before, but this night it was beautiful. Everything seemed different to me. It was raining softly and the city lights created a golden glow. Something had happened to me.' Now something had happened to Chuck too. He had never felt like this before.

Later that week Chuck had a visitor at his office. As soon as Chuck had asked Christ into his life he wrote to Tom Phillips to tell him and to thank him for his vital part in what had happened. Tom had wasted no time. He immediately contacted a Christian friend in Washington, Doug Coe, and now Doug was waiting to see Chuck. His secretary was suspicious of the tall, dark man in the crumpled raincoat who was asking to see Chuck. She assumed he was a reporter from a newspaper, trying to dig up more stories on Watergate. But Doug was nothing like the pushy men and women who had camped on Chuck and Patty's doorstep and called on the office so many times in the past year. One major difference was that he smiled all the time.

Doug organized prayer breakfasts and other Christian fellowship meetings in Washington and had been around the Senate for a long time. It was surprising that they had never met before, and Doug certainly greeted Chuck as if they were old friends. He flung an arm around Chuck's shoulders, then flopped down in a chair, completely at home. He explained that Tom had read Chuck's letter to him and asked him to get in touch. Chuck stiffened slightly. That letter to Tom was private. He did not want a complete stranger reading it. What was more his conversion had been something private too. But Doug was so sincerely warm and friendly that it suddenly did not seem to matter.

Soon Chuck was pouring out the whole story. Doug listened intently and his eyes glowed with warmth and compassion. When Chuck had finished, the enthusiastic Doug suggested he should meet another Christian in government – Harold Hughes.

Chuck was not so sure. Hughes was a Democrat and was strongly opposed to the Republicans and to the Vietnam War. Much to his surprise, however, Doug did not see this as a problem. Now that he was a Christian, there would be plenty of people all over Washington who would want to meet him and help him, Harold Hughes included. There were even men and women praying for him. Chuck was astonished and deeply moved. He had felt under siege during the past few months as prosecutors, committees, the press and, it seemed, half of Washington had been out to get him. Now, apparently, there were perfect strangers who cared for him and would support him. And Doug was right. Over the days that followed, while former colleagues were keeping their distance as the Watergate accusations hotted up, men whom Chuck scarcely knew came up to him and said the same: 'As brothers in Christ we stand together.'

Chuck, however, was not sure he was looking forward to meeting Harold Hughes, though the more he heard about Harold, the more fascinated he was by him. Harold had been a truck driver and an alcoholic and was often suicidally depressed. One night, in despair, he had prayed for help. The next day, when he awoke, everything had seemed different and new. He never touched alcohol again. Later he became involved in both the Church and politics and was elected Democratic Governor of Iowa, and in 1968, Senator. He threw himself into the campaign against the Vietnam War, making himself Chuck's enemy as he did so. He then started to campaign to be the Democratic Party's Presidential candidate for the 1972 elections. He later withdrew and in the summer of 1973 announced he would retire from the Senate in 1975. His decision was prompted by his Christian faith. He felt he could do more good outside the Senate than in.

While Chuck was fascinated by Harold, Harold certainly did not want to meet Chuck, telling Doug that he disliked Chuck more than anyone because of what he stood for. Doug, however, was firm about it, and eventually Harold agreed. The meeting was to take place at Republican Congressman Al Quie's home. To balance the politics, Doug also arranged for the Democrat Graham Purcell and his wife to join them. They were all Christians and it would be a chance for Chuck to experience Christian fellowship.

Patty drove Doug's wife Jan to the Quie's house so Chuck went with Doug. He was not expecting to find Harold in the front seat of the car with Doug. The journey was tense, with Harold scowling as he thought about Chuck sitting in the back. They were all relieved when they arrived.

The meeting was a strange, new experience for Chuck and Patty. They were used to cocktail parties where the talk was of politics, and where the politicians – usually men – boasted of their latest successes, leaving the women to talk among themselves. They were not used to the homeliness of the group of men and women sitting around chatting generally, drinking iced tea and eating apple pie. Chuck felt awkward, especially when Harold asked him to tell them about his conversion.

Chuck was nervous and he sensed that Patty was too. He hardly knew these people, and speaking about his faith was a new, difficult experience. He found, however, that he did not feel embarrassed, although he did wonder at one point if his audience would think he had gone mad. He was not expecting the response. First there was silence, then Harold said, 'That's all I need to know, Chuck. You have accepted Jesus and he has forgiven you. I do the same. I love you now as my brother in Christ. I will stand with you, defend you anywhere, and trust you with anything I have.'

'Thank you' was all that Chuck could bring himself to say. He was both very moved and astounded by what Harold had said. Later the others gathered round and pledged their support for him too. Only Patty was uncertain. She would stand by Chuck through anything, but she did not understand what was happening to him. She had her own faith, but her experience of Christianity did not include the type of fellowship she was witnessing that night. Chuck did not realize it at the time, but by using expressions like 'accepting Christ' which she did not use, he was alienating her.

After that night Chuck and Harold, Doug, Al and Graham continued to meet every Monday for breakfast at Fellowship House, a building in Washington where many groups of Christians gathered each week. Chuck drew enormous strength and comfort from these meetings, learning a great deal about Christian fellowship and forgiveness. They regularly prayed for Nixon, and, at Harold's suggestion, Chuck even asked Nixon if he would join them. He declined. They also asked Spiro Agnew, who had been forced to resign as Vice-

President as a result of charges of financial misdealings. Agnew felt the humiliation deeply and the small group wanted to offer him support and friendship. He too declined.

One day in December Chuck's new-found Christian fellowship brought him back into the White House. A group of Christians met regularly in the west wing of the White House for breakfast, prayer and Bible reading. Harold was invited to speak at one of their meetings and asked Chuck to come with him, since he was a little nervous of being in the midst of staunch Republican Nixon-supporters. Chuck knew a lot of the people there – old Republican allies he did not realize were Christians. He was not, however, expecting to see Arthur Burns.

Arthur, Chairman of the Federal Reserve Board, was an old friend of Nixon's but had once failed to support the President over an economic issue because he had disagreed with him. Chuck had, at Nixon's suggestion, put out a story to the press about Arthur, claiming that he was trying to raise his own salary when asking others to keep wages down. The report was not true and Arthur protested, clearing his own name. He later discovered that Chuck was the source of the story so he had good reason to dislike him.

Arthur was very surprised when Harold, speaking at the breakfast meeting, talked about Chuck and his new faith, explaining how he had hated Chuck and other men like him once, and how by hating he was shutting Christ's love out of his life. But now, Harold explained, he loved Chuck as if he were his own brother and trusted him completely. At the end Arthur, visibly moved, reached out to hold Chuck's hand and asked him to finish in prayer.

Chuck caught up with Arthur after the meeting and apologized for planting the story about him. 'You don't need to apologize,' replied Arthur. 'All that is behind us.' Then he added, a little hesitantly as if uncertain how to express himself, 'This has been quite a morning.'

It was quite a morning in more ways than one. News reporters had seen Chuck enter the White House that morning and at the regular White House press briefing one of them asked what Chuck had been doing there. The answer surprised them. They did not expect Chuck, whom many of them saw as a criminal, to be interested in prayer breakfasts. An hour later, Chuck's phone would not stop ringing. The press wanted to know what was going on. He tried to put them off, explaining that his religion was his own affair, not ready yet to speak about it to the world in general. But the story came out.

Chuck had been to the White House many times over the past few months, so why did the press pick today, he wondered, to ask why he was there? Perhaps God wanted him to speak about it, even though it was one of the last things he wanted to tell the press. Eventually Chuck decided to confirm what the reporters had already heard, since to deny it would be a denial of the wonderful changes in his life. He called the reporters back and told them.

The next day the papers were full of it: 'Colson, "Mr Tough Guy" Finds Christ' announced the front page of the *Washington Post,* and continued with, 'In some ways, the story is as startling as any of the other startling revelations which have come out of Watergate.' 'If Mr Colson can repent his sins, there just has to be hope for everybody,' said the *Boston Globe.* 'I cannot accept the sudden coming to Christ of Charles Colson,' wrote columnist Harriet Van Horne. On the whole, the announcement was greeted with cynicism; even the *Washington Post*'s sympathetic article concluded, with more than a touch of realism: 'Colson can practically hear them laughing all over Washington.'

Friends and family were confused by the announcement, not understanding. Others, including the Watergate prosecutors, thought that he had been prompted by guilt and would now want to confess to his part in the Watergate break-in and subsequent cover-up. Dave Shapiro thought that it would seem like a cry for sympathy and would do him no good.

Yet others were sympathetic and letters came in from supporters. One man wrote on Christmas Day to say that reading about his conversion had helped him to sort himself out and stop drinking, and that he was enjoying being with his children that Christmas: 'It's people in positions like you who confess their past . . . Sure do help people in a position like me. I truly feel free within my inner self this morning and I pray that God may help both of us in all of our trying efforts.' Reading this letter Chuck felt that everything he was going through was worthwhile.

CHAPTER NINE

Accusation and Decision

The new-found support for Chuck came at a time when he most needed it. In the early autumn of 1973 the grand jury investigating the break-in at the office of Dr Fielding, Ellsberg's psychiatrist, was hearing evidence on Chuck. A grand jury hears the evidence of Government prosecutors and decides whether or not there is enough evidence to merit a trial in court. Chuck thought that if he told the truth the jury would be sure to decide against a trial. Dave Shapiro was not so sure, but he agreed to Chuck's wishes. Later Chuck realized that Dave was right to have reservations.

The hearing was not a success. Chuck, who was used to representing people rather than answering questions put to him by hostile lawyers, was shaking with nerves as he heard the Special Prosecutor's Assistant Will Merrill say: 'I should tell you . . . that from evidence the grand jury has heard you are a prospective defendant in the violation of certain criminal statutes . . . that you therefore have the right to take the Fifth Amendment [the right to decline to answer] to any question I may give you, that any answers that you do give here can obviously be used against you.'[1]

Instead, however, of asking Chuck about the break-in at Fielding's office, Merrill asked Chuck questions about other 'dirty tricks' that he had been involved in during election campaigns. When he was finally asked about Ellsberg the jury did not seem particularly interested, and it soon became clear that he was not helping himself by answering questions. He gave up his appearances and two days later Chuck heard the news – he was going to be indicted, which meant he would have to stand trial.

When Chuck heard the news about the indictment he thought of Patty and his children and how they would feel. If he lost the trial he might go to prison. As a successful lawyer, prison was something that happened to other people – criminals he might even have helped to put there. Deep down he was also frightened about what would happen to him if he went to prison: as a member of Nixon's Government he might well be seen as an 'enemy' by some of the men inside. Some of these men were violent and dangerous and Chuck shuddered to think of what could happen to him. He had thought about prison in the past, when the Watergate accusations had first begun in earnest, but now, he realized, he did not feel the same dread and fear that he used to have about it. True, he did not welcome the idea of prison, but it no longer seemed the end of the world.

The fact that Chuck was likely to stand trial meant that his lawyers did not want him to appear before any more committees investigating Watergate or any other connected matter. The worry was that anything he said could be used against him in his trial later on so that he might not have a fair hearing.

In September, however, Chuck was summoned before the Ervin Committee which was investigating Watergate. Dave Shapiro argued that Chuck should not appear. The only testifying he should do was in court, otherwise he might undermine his case. The Committee, however, held firm in their summons, so Dave insisted on something else – that Chuck should take the Fifth Amendment. The Fifth Amendment allows American citizens the right to decline to answer questions put before them by investigating committees which might lead to self-incrimination, so preventing a fair trial later on.

Chuck was horrified. To him 'taking the Fifth' had always seemed like an admission of guilt. In any case, he wanted to testify and tell the truth. By telling what he knew of the truth he wanted to be the one to save his old boss to whom he remained deeply loyal, President Nixon. Dave, however, told him that he could find himself another lawyer if he did not take the Fifth. Reluctantly, Chuck agreed, telling the committee, 'I am going to follow the instructions of my counsel, which I have to say are not the instructions of my conscience.'[2] Then in answer to the questions put to him he said, hardly able to force out the words, 'I decline to answer.' The next day the press was full of the story. To them it seemed obvious: Chuck was guilty.

Chuck had to wait several months before he was indicted. Special Prosecutor Archibald Cox was fired and it took a while before the new prosecutor, Leon Jaworski, was in a position to continue at the same pace. This gave Chuck a chance to build up his faith, ready for the difficult times ahead. It also gave

Patty the time to think through her own beliefs. The way that Chuck expressed his faith was very different from the way she did, and she had been afraid that Chuck would want her to give up attending the Roman Catholic church where she went regularly, although nothing was further from Chuck's mind. She decided to join a Bible study course for women, and quietly her faith began to deepen and grow.

The first of Chuck's old colleagues to be indicted was Egil Krogh, who had been head of the Plumbers' Unit, set up to investigate and stop the leaking of Government secrets to the press. He had admitted to ordering the break-in at Dr Fielding's office, for reasons of 'national security', even though he had previously denied it under oath. Just before Christmas 1973 he had made the surprising decision to plead guilty in court, saying, 'I now feel that I cannot in conscience assert national security as a defence.' He was sentenced to six months in prison.

The sentencing shook Chuck up. He was still waiting for his indictment, but he did not really believe that he would have to go to prison. However, knowing that a former colleague was to be shut away for six months was an unnerving experience.

The week before Egil – known to his friends as Bud – was due to go to prison, Chuck, Harold, Doug, Al and Graham invited him to join them at Fellowship House. They wanted to show Bud that they cared for him and would stand by him. Chuck expected Bud to look careworn and dejected, but the man who arrived at Fellowship House seemed full of energy and enthusiasm.

Bud told them that he and his wife Suzanne had been studying the Bible and that they could even bring themselves to thank God for what was happening. Before the trial, Bud and Suzanne had been having marriage difficulties, but now they had overcome them and were stronger together than ever. They had little money and few prospects but, when they had prayed about how they were going to manage, Suzanne had been offered a teaching job at their children's school.

Chuck marvelled at Bud and Suzanne's faith. He hoped that if the time ever came for him to be imprisoned he would have the same strength. Bud had also had the strength not to agree to a plea bargain, which would have enabled him to plead guilty to a lesser crime which carried a shorter sentence in return for testifying against other people. He had decided to do what he believed was right.

Soon Chuck was faced with the same dilemma. Jaworski told him that there did not seem to be enough evidence against him to merit an indictment over the Watergate case but that there was always the Fielding break-in. Jaworski then hinted that if he pleaded guilty to conspiring to burgle Fielding's office to find evidence to use against Daniel Ellsberg, and offered testimony about some of his former colleagues, he would get a light sentence, possibly probation, and be able to continue practising law. If, however, he did not plea bargain, he might be tried for a more serious crime – the Watergate cover-up – perhaps be sent to prison and not be allowed to practise law again.

It was tempting, very tempting. Chuck was being offered the chance to get his life back to normal again. But he wondered whether he would be strong enough to testify absolutely truthfully. If he did not give the prosecutors the information they wanted, they would not be so lenient with him. If they asked him about one of his colleagues and clearly wanted a certain answer, even if it were not the true answer, would Chuck be strong enough to resist the temptation?

He turned to Patty and Harold for help. Harold, uncertain what he would do in the same situation, asked Chuck whether what he would have to say in court would be true. Chuck thought for a while. When Nixon had asked him to expose Ellsberg he would have done anything to harm his position with the public, but he had not known about the break-in at the psychiatrist's office so he could not say that he had. He could not therefore plead guilty to it. Slowly he let this realization sink in. He could not plea bargain and sadly he told Harold this. Patty agreed with him reluctantly, seeing the chances of a normal life slipping away again.

Chuck told Jaworski his decision and the wait began again to see if he would be indicted. On Friday 1 March 1974 the news came – Chuck was indicted with six others in the Watergate cover-up case; he would also be indicted in the Ellsberg case.

The enormity of what had happened did not sink in at the time, but eight days later Chuck appeared in court to hear the charges. With him were John

Mitchell, Nixon's campaign manager; Bob Haldeman, Nixon's Chief of Staff; John Ehrlichman, Nixon's Chief Domestic aide; Kenneth Parkinson, a CRP lawyer; Robert Mardian, Mitchell's former aide; and Gordon Strachan, Haldeman's assistant. Gordon Strachan was only twenty-seven and had become caught up in the Watergate case because of his loyalty to Haldeman. Now he was confused and nearly in tears. Chuck longed to comfort him, promising to talk to him when they could.

The judge, John Sirica, summoned them forward and said, 'The United States of America charges . . . Charles Colson . . .' At these words the awfulness of the situation sunk in. Chuck was deeply patriotic and the thought that his beloved country was charging him with a criminal act, with failing in his duty and trust, made him feel sick with shame and horror. Struggling, his mouth dry and his words almost inaudible, Chuck managed to reply, 'Not guilty to all counts.'

Full of shame and fear, understanding now what it felt like to be an individual with the power of the Government against him, Chuck thought of St Paul and his words to the Romans: 'Neither death, nor life, nor angels, nor principalities, nor powers can separate us from Jesus.' (Romans 8:38-39) In his despair Chuck clung onto those words and felt Jesus with him, caring for him and supporting him.

Chuck's brothers in Christ, as he had come to see them, were also supportive. Remaining loyal to Chuck could have damaged their own reputations and their futures in politics and law, but when Chuck offered to withdraw from the fellowship they were horrified. They would stand with him, whatever happened.

Chuck did, however, withdraw from his law firm. Dave and his partners set about organizing his defence case. The Ellsberg trial would be held in July and the Watergate one in September. There would not be time to prepare properly for both, so Dave and the others tried to delay the trials. One way of doing this was to persuade the judges that public opinion was so strongly convinced that those indicted in the two trials were guilty that it would be impossible to find an impartial jury. Ken Adams, an associate lawyer at the firm, suggested collecting every newspaper article published in the past two years which accused Chuck of anything and giving them to the judges. This would show the amount of prejudice against Chuck. It was a mammoth task: with some eighty Christian volunteers to help, four copies each of thousands of newspaper clippings – bound into books stacked in piles seven feet high – were ready to submit as evidence to the court two weeks later. The judges, however, rejected the evidence. But for Chuck the exercise had been worth it: the volunteers had brought love and joy to the law firm's offices.

As the trial drew nearer Chuck felt torn in two. His lawyers were telling him not to testify in the impeachment hearings against Nixon, and at the trial not to say anything that would damage his own case. Chuck longed to tell the truth about whatever he was asked by the prosecutors. He felt that the old Chuck Colson was on trial and that he did not want to defend the way the old Chuck had behaved.

One day, he and Harold Hughes were asked to appear on *Sixty Minutes*, a television show which would be watched by twenty million people. The host was a fearsome broadcaster called Mike Wallace. They talked about the tapes that Nixon had, recording meetings in the Oval Office. Chuck was not proud of the conversations they had had. They did not reveal Nixon and his men – Chuck included – as pleasant people. Chuck, however, did not want to make any judgements about them. He might have to answer questions about them in court so he knew it was best to keep quiet. Frustrated by this, Wallace said, 'You say that you are a new man in Jesus Christ. It seems as though your prior faith takes precedence over your new faith.'

Chuck was stung. He knew Wallace was right. He could not be a criminal defendant and a Christian disciple at the same time. What was more, although he was innocent of the charges of knowing about the break-in at Dr Fielding's offices in advance, the thought kept coming back to him that, when he had heard about it, he had judged it was justified. He had been so caught up in the belief that almost anything was justified to protect the Government against Daniel Ellsberg that he had never thought of Ellsberg's rights as an individual.

He thought back to something he had read in C. S. Lewis's *Mere Christianity*: 'If individuals live only seventy years, then a state, or a nation, or a civilization which may last for a thousand years is more important than an individual. But if Christianity is true, then the individual is not only more important but incomparably more important, for he is everlasting and the life of a state or civilization, compared with his, is only a moment.'[3] Daniel Ellsberg's rights were more important than protecting the State. The fact that he did not know about the Fielding break-in beforehand was irrelevant. Chuck believed he was guilty of trying to smear Ellsberg in order to protect the Government.

His feelings of guilt were confirmed when he spoke at a prayer breakfast in Owosso, Michigan. A slip of the tongue made him say, 'I know in my own heart that I am innocent of many of the charges . . .' Suddenly he realized what he had said. Why *many* of the charges and not *all* of them? He recovered quickly and no one seemed to have noticed, but it was a final turning point for Chuck. He could not, he felt, live a full Christian life while he was still defending his own behaviour as a member of the White House staff. He wanted to put it all behind him and if that meant pleading guilty and going to prison, then that was what he would do. He would plead guilty to a charge which had not been brought against him – that of trying to find and publicize information about Ellsberg which would under-mine him and destroy his image and his chances of a fair hearing when he was standing trial. He assumed that this would mean that the other charges would be dropped, though he could not be absolutely sure.

Relieved, Chuck went home to face the task of telling Patty and his Christian brothers. This would hit them all very hard.

Notes

1 Transcript of the grand jury proceedings.
2 From the Executive Session transcripts of the Ervin Committee.
3 C. S. Lewis, *Mere Christianity*, op. cit.

CHAPTER TEN

Pleading Guilty

'Why? Why do you have to do it?' Patty was devastated when Chuck told her that he wanted to plead guilty. 'Dave says you'll be acquitted. Then our lives will be normal again.' Patty fought but failed to hold back her tears. She had supported Chuck all along, but why did he now have to throw away his chances of a normal life? They talked late into the night as Chuck tried to persuade her that he had to do this; that this was the only way that their lives would get better, however much it hurt. He knew how much this was hurting Patty and how much pain it would cause her in the future. It was a devastating thing to have to ask of her. Eventually, after much heart searching and tears, she agreed to trust that Chuck knew what he was doing.

The news hurt Harold, Doug, Al and Graham too. Graham found it particularly hard to accept. He had been a judge in Texas and knew something of the horrors of the prisons in which he had sentenced men and women to spend time. He was not sure Chuck's faith should be calling him to this, but when Chuck remained calmly adamant he eventually and sadly agreed.

Dave Shapiro was a different case. He went wild and shouted at Chuck down the telephone, telling him he was mad and that he could not plead guilty to something that, in his opinion, was not a crime. Chuck was not to be swayed. He was going to plead guilty and that was all there was to it. He asked Dave to contact the prosecutors and Judge Gesell, who was hearing the Ellsberg cases, and tell them what he was doing, stressing that he was expecting no special treatment and no deals.

'Are you sure you know what you're doing?' Patty, then Dave asked Chuck on the following Monday morning. Chuck was certain, more certain than he had ever been about anything in his life. What was uncertain was whether the judge would agree to accept Chuck's plea, since no one in the past had ever been charged with the crime of sending out derogatory information about a criminal defendant. Chuck said it ought to be a crime and the plea would set an important precedent.

Judge Gesell was on a week's holiday at the time and would make no decision until he was back. For the next week Dave researched the background to the plea, unconvinced it was a crime but convinced now that Chuck meant business and therefore still needed a good lawyer. Meanwhile, Chuck and Patty lived with the suspense of not knowing what would happen, either in the short term – whether Judge Gesell would agree to the plea – or in the long term – whether Chuck would go to prison, and if so, how they would cope. If the judge did not accept his plea it would probably harm Chuck's position in the later court cases, making it look as if he had been trying to bargain his way out of more serious charges.

Patty tried her best to be supportive to Chuck, but

she was very frightened. The two had never been apart for more than a couple of days in all the years of their marriage and the separation would be tough on both of them. The strain on prisoners' families is often ignored as they struggle to keep a normal home life going during a prison sentence. Their thoughts about the dangers of prison remained unspoken, but they prayed silently together, bringing all their fears to God.

Just after nine o'clock on Monday morning, 3 June, Chuck sat in his office nervously waiting for the telephone to ring and the message to come through from Dave Shapiro. Patty was waiting too, trying to talk normally but with her stomach churning and her attention fixed on the telephone. It seemed an age before it rang, though they had to wait little more than ten minutes. Dave called to say that Gesell would accept his plea and Chuck was to appear in court straightaway.

There was one final telephone call to be made before going to court – to President Nixon. Nixon was in a meeting, but Chuck passed on an urgent message telling Nixon that, although he was pleading guilty, he was not betraying him. Chuck was determined to remain loyal to his old friend, the man he had admired so much.

Finally Chuck was in the courtroom. His heart was beating fast and his legs felt weak. Will Merrill read out the charge: that Chuck was responsible for a plan to 'defame and destroy Mr Ellsberg's public image . . . to influence, obstruct and impede the conduct and outcome of the Ellsberg trial'. Even though Chuck had written those words, they sounded terrible to him. He had to keep holding on to the thought that by this action he would be free from the past. The press were stunned and excited. It would make a great story – the first of Nixon's closest advisers to fall.

Shakily Chuck made his statement: 'I have come to believe in the very depths of my being that official threats to the right of fair trial for defendants such as those charged in this information must be stopped; and by this plea, Your Honour, I am prepared to take whatever consequences I must to help in stopping them.' With this, Chuck pleaded guilty. Now all he had to wait for was sentencing on 21 June.

Chuck was escorted to a small probation room, a convicted criminal. The enormity of what he had done began to sink in. Then Doug Coe appeared at the door and waved to him. Chuck could not hold back his emotions any longer. It meant so much to have friends like Doug – always there when they were most needed.

Chuck was glad in many ways that sentencing was to be so soon, since he knew that he would be called as a witness in the forthcoming Watergate trials. He wanted to be sentenced first so that what he said would not be influenced in any way by the thought of possibly gaining a lighter sentence. However, it did not give him and his lawyers much time to collect together letters and recommend-ations asking for leniency.

In the following days Chuck and Patty went through many highs and lows. Chuck was particularly worried about his father, who was recovering from a second heart attack and on whom the shame of Chuck's prison sentence would fall hard. He was also concerned for his children and the way their classmates and other friends would treat them.

No one could guess what sentence Judge Gesell would impose. Sometimes Chuck would think, 'Could he give me a suspended sentence?' He hardly dared to hope it. Letters were, however, flooding in to the judge urging him to be lenient. Patty was banking on – and praying for – a suspended sentence, and Dave Shapiro, who had worked so hard to defend Chuck over the past months, was feeling optimistic. He thought that Chuck would receive six months. Chuck tried to be realistic. With two weeks to go before sentencing day, another man accused in the Watergate scandal – former Attorney General Richard Kleindienst – was given a suspended sentence. The press were outraged and called for longer sentences in the future. Chuck would be the next Watergate man to hear the judge's gavel fall. Judge Gesell was known as the fairest judge on the bench, but might he be influenced by the calls?

There were some high spots in those days. Chuck's action had meant that many of his former staff were no longer being investigated by the prosecutors and he rejoiced for them. One day, too, he found an unexpected opportunity to talk about his conversion. He was asked to appear before a probation officer who would then make a report to the judge. The meeting could help to lighten his sentencing, but even if it did not achieve that it seemed to help the probation officer. The officer wanted to hear about Chuck's conversion and listened intently as he spoke, not because he wanted details for the report but because he wanted to know for himself what had made such a difference to Chuck's life. It turned out that he was a former alcoholic and Chuck was able to put him in touch with Harold Hughes.

As 21 June drew nearer Chuck's family and friends gathered round him, offering support and sorting out some of the practical problems which would result from Chuck's imprisonment. Doug Coe's daughter and a friend offered to come and stay with Patty since the Colson's house was isolated, surrounded by trees. Others offered Patty a place to stay, a spare car, cash. Even columnist Jack Anderson, who had long criticized Chuck, quietly offered Patty financial help just moments before he and Chuck were to debate with each other on television. Like many of the others who offered help, Jack had a deep faith. So once again Chuck was experiencing Christian love in action.

Patty and Chuck went to visit Bud and Suzanne Krogh. Bud had just come out of prison and Chuck was anxious to find out what prison was like and how it had affected Bud. Chuck was surprised to find how little changed Bud seemed at first. He looked the same strong, determined person, except for one thing – he did not seem interested in the world around him. He was distant and withdrawn about anything other than prison or his family. This worried Chuck. He did not want the same thing to happen to him.

Bud described some of the horrors he had had to

cope with. He had once seen a man having his head smashed in by other prisoners. He had also spent almost a fortnight in Montgomery County Jail, crushed into one cell with eleven other men. There was nowhere to sleep except for the floor and Bud had to lie next to the toilet. One night a man urinated all over him. Chuck knew that much the same was in store for him. Most of all, however, he worried that he too would feel cut off from the world.

All too soon sentencing day arrived. Chuck and Patty were up early and down at the courtroom not long after nine o'clock. Chuck felt sick with nerves and his palms were clammy. At least, he told himself, the suspense will soon be over. The court was packed with friends, colleagues and well-wishers, so much so that there was hardly room for the press. Everyone was tense.

Dave Shapiro was preparing for his last-ditch attempt at persuading Judge Gesell to change his mind. He had planned a magnificent speech, a passionate plea which outlined all the false accusations made against Chuck. Further, it claimed that if Chuck were sent to prison it would be because that was what the public wanted – hardly a just reason for imposing a sentence.

The door opened and Judge Gesell marched in, a dignified but angry-looking figure. Chuck's heart sank. Gesell may have been known to be fair, but it was also said that if he were angry then it was bad news for the defendant. Chuck and Dave went forward. Chuck explained why he was pleading guilty, finishing with the words: 'I can assure the court that this experience has brought me to a complete re-examination of my life. I regret what I have done and I will spend a lifetime trying to be a better man as a result.'

Then it was Dave's turn. He launched into his speech, dramatically exclaiming how unfair the indictments were, how many false things Chuck had been accused of by the public and the press, how even the CIA had placed false stories about him in the newspapers. But Judge Gesell was not to be persuaded. In fact, he had already made up his mind. 'I am not,' he said, 'a bit interested in the public expectations . . . you are beating a dead horse.' Dave was shattered, but for Chuck it was worse. With a nauseous, sinking sensation in the pit of his stomach he knew for sure that he would be going to prison – it was simply a case of finding out how long. The maximum sentence would be five years.

There was silence in the courtroom as Gesell once again summoned Chuck and Dave to the lectern. Chuck tried to calm himself, breathing slowly, and Dave put his arm around Chuck's back to support him and give him strength. Then Gesell began to speak of Chuck's 'deliberate misconduct [affecting] the conduct of a pending federal prosecution'. Then, at last, he said, 'The court will impose a sentence of one to three years and a fine of $5,000.' The gavel came down with a crash.

CHAPTER ELEVEN

Convicted Criminal

'What happened in court today was the court's will and the Lord's will. I have committed my life to Jesus Christ and I can work for him in prison as well as out.' Chuck faced the press on the steps of the courthouse, surrounded by Patty, his Christian brothers and his son Wendell. He did not know what to say; he hardly knew what to think or how he felt, apart from being numb. But he prayed for the Holy Spirit to speak for him and heard himself saying those words.

Chuck and Patty had only a few days left together now for Chuck was to start his sentence on 8 July. The minimum time he would be in prison was a year, after which he would be eligible for parole; the maximum was three years. The days of freedom went by all too fast. Chuck had been worried about how Patty would stand up to the pressure, but her faith seemed to deepen all the time and he had been surprised at how strong and brave she was. They tried to treat every day like any other, enjoying each one to the full and spending time with their family and friends.

Finally 8 July arrived. Chuck was woken by the sound of crunching gravel outside. His first sleepy thought was 'What's that noise?' His next thought was accompanied by a sinking feeling in the pit of his stomach: today he was to go to prison and leave Patty and the home he loved behind.

The noises outside came from the press, who wanted a few good quotes from him for their newspapers and television reports. Chuck was determined to have a peaceful last few hours with Patty. He persuaded the reporters to leave them alone until he was due to leave. By the early afternoon reporters and camera operators had filled the gateway to Chuck and Patty's drive. Going to prison had one benefit perhaps, thought Chuck wryly – no press.

Graham had offered to drive Chuck to Baltimore where the marshals would meet him and drive him to Fort Holabird. He would be held there while he was needed to testify at Watergate trials. The other charges against him had been dropped, but he was still viewed as an important witness. At around two o'clock Chuck and Patty heard Graham's large car draw up in the drive. The moment had come. As they left the house Chuck closed the front door behind him with a feeling of great sadness. He would not see his home for at least another year. He would not wake up with Patty, have quiet meals with her, visit friends with her or go to the coast with her. He would not swim in the pool or have a bath in his own bathroom. He would miss all the comforts, but most of all he would miss the love and fellowship of Patty and his friends. His heart felt as if it were being wrenched in two.

They climbed into Graham's car and headed off towards the cluster of press men and women at the gate. The press in their turn leapt into their own cars and followed Graham as he turned out of the drive. They pursued the car through the streets of Washington to a motel in Baltimore where Chuck was to meet the marshals. The press were even there to take pictures when he said goodbye to Patty, not allowing them a last moment's privacy. As the cameras clicked, Chuck was bundled into an unmarked car. He turned round to wave one last time to Patty and Graham, both bravely trying to smile but hardly able to hold back their emotions. Then the car's engine roared and Chuck was off, a prisoner of the State.

Fort Holabird was an army-style barracks on a deserted army base, a prison where criminals were held when they were required to testify in other trials. They drove through the eerily empty base until they came to a green wooden building surrounded by a high fence. Two armed men unlocked the gates and Chuck was told to get out of the car. The marshals escorted him through the gate which slammed behind him with a terrible crash. There was no way out now.

Inside the prison the heat was almost unbearable. Chuck was escorted down a long corridor lit by dim, bare light bulbs, past a small kitchen which exuded a sickening greasy smell and into a glassed-in office called the Control Room. Here they went through Chuck's belongings, searched him for drugs, took his picture and fingerprints, and filled out official forms.

Chuck made the mistake of being friendly, asking about the prison. 'The important thing to remember is that you remember nothing,' snapped the deputy in charge of him. 'No one knows this place exists. You will meet some very unusual men here. Don't discuss your business with them and don't ask them about theirs. When you leave, forget you ever met them.'

The 'unusual men', it turned out, were mainly Mafia men, heroin traffickers, conmen, hitmen (including one who had killed twenty-eight people), even a couple of ex-policemen on corruption charges. Many of their own lives were under threat, and the police wanted to keep them safe to use them as witnesses. They were a tough group and sometimes Chuck felt fearful, wishing he could lock his door at night. Surprisingly, the doors to their tiny rooms did not lock. Something else that Chuck found surprising was that the prisoners – or 'principals' as they were called there – did all their own cooking, housekeeping and cleaning. The food was remarkably good, all things considered.

He also found some friendship there. First there was Herbert Kalmbach, Nixon's personal lawyer, who had been sent to the prison the week before after the unpleasant experience of being thrown into Los Angeles County Jail, a fate that Chuck was glad to have escaped. Later they were joined by two more Watergate men: John Dean, former Counsel to the President, and Jeb Magruder, former Deputy Campaign Director for the Committee to Re-elect the President.

Chuck had felt a great deal of anger towards John Dean who had testified against Nixon to the Ervin Committee. He could not believe that John was telling the truth about Nixon, whom Chuck had respected as both a leader and a friend. Chuck's anger had lessened, but he did not know how easy he would find it to love John, as his faith told him he should. When John arrived in September, however, Chuck heard that he was to be confined to his room, isolated from the others in case he discussed the Watergate case with them. This thought made Chuck feel compassion for John, and, before the marshall could stop them, Chuck and Herb Kalmbach approached John and welcomed him as a friend. From then on, when the guard outside John's room could be persuaded to let them talk, Chuck and the others would drop by and chat.

John was grateful for this friendship and also noticed a marked change in Chuck. They had not seen each other since Chuck had become a Christian. In his book *Blind Ambition*, John later wrote: 'There was something real about the new Chuck Colson, I decided after a period of scepticism. He was different, but his faith did not erase his old zest or wit. "Sometimes I don't think there's much ministry for me to do in here," he twinkled one night. "All these Mafia guys say they're already good Catholics." '[1]

Chuck missed Patty desperately. He was allowed two personal telephone calls a week, as well as an unlimited number to his lawyer. Patty and the brothers visited when they could, but there was little privacy and the times together could be tense. One day, much to Chuck's joy, Patty wrote to suggest that they should pray together. From then on they held hands and prayed during each visit. Both found how much this helped them to keep going. Patty did her best for Chuck in other ways too. She even appeared on the *Today* show on television for him, talking about the possibility of his being pardoned.

Nixon resigned on 8 August 1974 and on 8 September the new President, Gerald Ford, granted him a full pardon. It was difficult for Chuck and the others, who had gone to prison or were being tried for crimes they had committed on Nixon's behalf. Rumours began circulating that the Watergate prisoners would be pardoned too. Patty not only had to put up with being on a television show – something she was not accustomed to – but also with a new batch of reporters camped outside her house , cameras poised in anticipation of capturing Chuck's homecoming. She and Chuck and the other prisoners and families were full of hope for the future, but these hopes were cruelly dashed when President Ford announced that there would be no more pardons.

That hot summer Chuck endured another grief. One day, Chuck's father Wendell had been preparing to visit his son in prison, even though warned against travelling because of poor health. Wendell and Chuck's mother Inez were packing their suitcases when Wendell suffered another, this time fatal, heart attack. He died peacefully in Inez's arms. Patty broke the news to Chuck later that morning and the two held each other tightly as he struggled with his feelings. He was choked up with sadness and remorse that his father had died knowing that Chuck was in prison.

Chuck was allowed to leave prison to help his

mother and Patty sort through his father's belongings, and to attend the small, private funeral held at St John's Episcopal Church in Winthrop, where Wendell Colson had been baptized. In the few days he was allowed out of prison he learned something about his father that he had never known before. Wendell had been involved in prison reform work, helping prisoners back in the 1930s. Chuck hoped that in the future he would be able to continue some of the work which his father had begun all those years ago.

Fort Holabird was unpleasant and at times frightening, but worse was to come for Chuck. Late that summer he was transferred to Maxwell Airbase prison camp in Alabama. Maxwell was a far tougher prison and much further from home than Holabird, which was hard on Patty. There were 250 prisoners there, whereas at Holabird there had been just twenty-one. Chuck was also stripped of more of his identity and privacy than before. As prisoner 23226 he was not allowed to keep many personal effects, not even his pictures of Patty and the children or the ring Patty had given him.

The officer in charge of clothing ignored the cross and dove which Chuck wore on a chain around his neck. He was not, however, allowed to keep any of his own clothes, but was made to strip naked and was then given prison clothing, including a well-worn pair of underpants. Chuck tried not to think about the number of men who must have worn them before. He was simply relieved to put them on to hide his nakedness. Chuck, now dressed in dull brown Air Force surplus work clothes, the trousers a couple of inches too short, was escorted across the prison compound to his dormitory.

He had been assigned to Dormitory G, where he would live with forty other men. Here he had a steel bed with a worn mattress, a metal night stand and a small locker where he could lock away the few personal possessions he had been allowed to keep. Chuck entered the dormitory and caught his breath. The air was stale with the smell of sweat and cigarette smoke. He would, he supposed, become used to it, but for the moment it felt suffocating. A large fan rotated slowly on the ceiling but it did little to relieve the oppressive atmosphere. Chuck stared at the four rows of beds separated only by night stands, then at the far end of the long room where there was an open toilet area. There would be no privacy here.

Chuck was summoned to the warden's office for an introductory talk. While he was waiting outside a tall man with glasses approached him and shook his hand. He was another prisoner, called 'Doc' Krenshaw, a doctor who had been convicted of fraud. Doc was friendly and gave him some advice he had heard before – not to get involved. The advice worried him because he did not want to become like Bud, cut off and distant from the world around him. Yet it seemed that this was how prisoners survived.

The other prisoners treated Chuck warily. He was a former Government official and therefore viewed by some of them as being 'on the other side'. He had been advised to find a prisoner who came from the country and talk to him, since this would break down some barriers. Across the dormitory was a friendly-looking man named Jed, and Chuck plucked up the courage to walk across to him and begin a conversation. They had a long and interesting talk about Jed's life in the mountains and Chuck found that the next day many of the other prisoners were less suspicious of him.

The first few days at Maxwell were disorientating and disturbing. Chuck did not sleep well, unused to sharing a room with forty other men; and waking when a guard came through every two hours, shining a torch to check that everyone was there. He could also hear scrabbling and flapping noises – the rats and cockroaches which shared the prison with them. Above all, he was struck by how little dignity prisoners could maintain.

Chuck began to find some sort of acceptance among the prisoners. All inmates had to do jobs, ranging from working on the nearby airbase, to clearing up the rubbish, to office duties. The warden had hinted that he could ask for an easy office job, but Chuck did not want to be given any favours which the other men would not be offered. In the end he was put to work in the laundry alongside Doc Krenshaw, sorting and washing sweaty clothes in sweltering heat. It was not a pleasant job but it was not the worst, and the fact that he had not received special treatment improved his standing with the other prisoners.

Not all the inmates accepted him, however. When he had been there less than a week another prisoner, Jerry, whispered that he wanted to see him. They walked away from the other men until they were sure they could not be overheard. Then Jerry gave him some news that made him feel sick. Chuck had an enemy in prison, someone who hated him so much that he wanted to kill him. Jerry would not say more than that; he simply warned him to be on his guard.

Chuck tried to appear calm while inside he was in a turmoil. Should he tell the guards? he wondered. It could be a test to see if he would do just that. If he did tell them, they might transfer him to another prison and he would be accused of having special treatment; or worse, he might be put in a maximum security prison and watched all the time. He shuddered at the thought. In the end Chuck decided that he could turn to only one source for help – God. That night he prayed for Christ's protection. But he slept fitfully, afraid that someone was slipping through the shadows towards his bed, weapon in hand.

Chuck felt very alone in prison and was missing the Christian fellowship he had been used to. Every Tuesday evening a local Baptist preacher, Brother Edmon Blow, took a small service in the auditorium. A red vinyl-covered altar was wheeled in, on top of which was a steel cross, with, Chuck noticed with amusement, the words 'US Government' imprinted on it. These services were more lively and full of loud praise for God than anything the rather reserved Chuck had been used to, but he found himself enjoying them immensely. Still, however, he longed to talk and pray with other Christians during the rest of the week.

He had noticed that one of the men in Dormitory

G wore a silver cross around his neck. Chuck decided to approach him. Paul Kramer was a young ex-marine, just twenty-seven years old. He had had money and marriage problems and had started to use and sell drugs. Four months later he was arrested and sentenced to three years in prison. In despair, in Texarkana Prison, he had turned to God and accepted Christ into his life. He arrived at Maxwell a short time before Chuck.

Chuck asked him if he thought they could start a little group in prison, with the idea of meeting and praying together a couple of times a week. Paul was not sure it was a good idea, but they decided to pray about it. So they stood together in the darkness outside the dormitory and prayed that God would bring men together in prison.

In the meantime he had visits from Patty to cheer him every Saturday and Sunday. It was a terrible strain for them being apart during the week and very painful when Patty had to leave on Sunday evening, but the visits helped to keep them both going.

Doug Coe's gift of a Bible study course also gave him a purpose. The first day's readings were from Hebrews 2, where the writer talks of Christ's sufferings and how he became a human to share in our suffering and humanity:

For the one who makes men holy and the men who are made holy share a common humanity. So that he is not ashamed to call them brothers. . . . It was imperative that he should be made like his brothers in every respect, if he were to become a high priest, both compassionate and faithful in the things of God . . . For by virtue of his own suffering under temptation he is able to help those who are exposed to temptation. (2:11, 17-18)

As Chuck read this passage, he felt sure that God was speaking to him. Two thoughts struck him. The first was that Jesus had come to earth so that we could know God as a brother through him. Jesus knew that men and women needed help and support through all the sufferings, fears and temptations they faced, so when he left the earth he gave us the Holy Spirit to be the source of God's strength and power with us. Chuck's second thought was that if God became human in order to understand our sufferings, then perhaps he, Chuck, had become a prisoner to understand how it really felt to be a sinner in prison. God, he thought, was asking him to call the other men in prison his brothers and to love them. He could never have understood the hardships and indignities of prison life as a mere prison visitor. And if God wanted him to love his fellow prisoners, then he would have to get involved with them, despite the advice given him by Bud, Doc Krenshaw and others.

Note

1 John Dean, *Blind Ambition*, op. cit.

CHAPTER TWELVE

Getting Involved

Chuck pondered over the question of getting involved. His limited experience of prison life already told him that involvement with other men's business could be dangerous. One evening he jumped between two men who were fighting and it was only his, untrue, warning that a guard was outside that saved him from the two men turning on him instead of each other.

Moreover, prison regulations forbade him giving legal advice to other prisoners, something he knew many of the men needed. The more Chuck knew of the other men's stories, the more he wondered about the injustices which had crept into the legal system. Many men had done serious wrong and deserved punishment, but sometimes their punishment seemed to outweigh their crime by a long way. Often those with little education and knowledge of the system suffered the most. They did not know how to appeal or how to fight for their rights. This fact came home to him one day early on in his time at Maxwell.

In the bed next to him was Homer Welsh, a shy, elderly man who always called Chuck 'sir'. He had been a labourer in coal mines in Tennessee, but also made illegal whisky or 'moonshine'. Moonshining is illegal, but an accepted practice in many rural areas and not seen as immoral. Many judges do not send moonshiners to prison. Homer was a hard-working, devout man who read his Bible every evening yet had ended up in prison unexpectedly. The judge had told him that he would be there for only four months, but the four months had passed and Homer had been unable to see his caseworker. He had a job lined up for November if he could get out in time. One evening he tentatively approached Chuck and asked if he could help him write a letter to the judge, asking if he could sort out the sentence.

Chuck liked Homer and knew that he could not afford a lawyer and probably would not know how to go about finding one in any case. He also knew that Homer needed a job and money. But he did not think he should break the regulations by helping him. Sadly he refused, and an apologetic but disappointed Homer returned to his own bed.

That night Chuck worried about Homer and the effect that prison was having on him and his family. He thought of a possible solution. If Homer outlined a letter to the judge, Chuck could look at it and suggest improvements. That way he would hardly be using his skills as a lawyer to help. In the morning he told Homer of the plan. He agreed readily and for the next week Chuck watched him as he sat on his bed writing. Eventually, Chuck asked him how he was getting on, imagining that he would be given several pages of information about Homer's case. Instead the old man brought out a sheet of paper with half a page of nearly illegible words. It was the best he could manage. Horrified, Chuck realized that although Homer could read, he could write very little and could not bring himself to say so.

There was nothing for it but to break the regulations and help. He took Homer off to the library and they drafted a letter in less than half an hour. The next day the letter was in the post. From then on, Chuck was available to help his fellow prisoners in their appeals. He was convinced that this was what God wanted him to do.

Sometimes he could scarcely believe the treatment some of the men had received. There was, for instance, a young man from North Carolina who had cashed a government pay cheque for a customer at his car repair garage. It turned out that the cheque had been stolen and, although he had nothing to do with it, the young man was given a six-month jail sentence. Then there was Dan, another young man, who came from Tennessee. He was so confused by his treatment in the courts that he did not know either what his sentence was or of what he had been convicted. It turned out that he had received a four-year sentence for buying a stolen car. It seemed that his court-appointed lawyer had negotiated a quick guilty plea with the prosecutors. Chuck agreed to help him plead his case with the judge.

There were other injustices, too, within the prison itself. One man in Maxwell with them, Jim Howard, was clearly near a nervous breakdown. There was no doctor in the prison apart from Krenshaw, who was forbidden to practise medicine, and the prison paramedic did nothing about it. Chuck longed to help, but Doc Krenshaw again warned him against getting involved. Then an opportunity arrived. It was Chuck's forty-third birthday and his old friends and law partners Charlie Morin and George Fender came to visit him.

As lawyers, Charlie and George were allowed to visit during the week. Because the visiting yard was closed they were shown to a room called the Captain's Office. Chuck was sure that the room was bugged and told Charlie so in a note. This meant that their conversation was rather stilted until Chuck had an idea. He started to talk about Jim Howard, saying how terrible it was that nobody cared what happened to him, and that he would probably die or commit suicide. 'The warden is so concerned with providing slave labour to the Air Force he doesn't think about individuals. I can't do anything about it now, but I sure will when I get out of here.' The next day Jim Howard was transferred to a prison hospital in Atlanta.

Prison morale was also affected by what happened to the men who were due for parole. Every two months parole hearings took place at Maxwell and men could have their sentences cut. As a lawyer on the outside, Chuck had assumed that parole was given almost automatically as long as the prisoner had behaved in prison. His first few weeks at Maxwell taught him differently. One Monday some parole examiners arrived at Maxwell to see twelve men. By the end of the day only two of the men had been granted parole and the atmosphere in the prison was tense and dark. Chuck was depressed by what he had heard. It seemed that many of the men had been denied parole because of regulations and guidelines, not because of any misbehaviour on their part.

Chuck decided to go to the small prison library to work that evening. He sat in one of the cramped writing booths and tried to write some letters. Other men were sitting around tables in the room chatting, reading or playing cards. A small group of men were gathered around Paul Kramer in the corner of the room. Chuck overheard them talking about a young prisoner called Bob who was desperate for parole. He and his wife had five children and no money – above all else Bob wanted to get out of prison and help them. But with what had happened at the parole hearings that day, there seemed little hope of this. Bob was in despair.

One of the men in the group, Tex, was suggesting that they should get together and pray with Bob. Tex was a former evangelist who had found that there was more money in buying and selling stolen cars. He had been caught and sent to prison where he had recommitted his life to Christ. Hearing him speaking about prayer, Chuck got up and joined them, offering to pray with Bob as well. Tex and his three companions were delighted and went to fetch Bob and a friend of Paul's called Amos. Paul was library clerk and had a key to some classrooms off the library, so the seven men settled down in one of them to pray.

Bob said nothing, but his eyes were filled with fear and anxiety. One of the men read from the Bible and then they prayed. Tex, crying out to God, asked him for mercy for the men who would go before the parole board the following day. On his knees he both begged God and praised him, loudly and exuberantly, and Chuck had no trouble picturing him as a fervent evangelist in the heart of the country. It was a tremendous evening and Bob was in tears by the end.

The next day seven men went before the parole board and five, including Bob, received parole. Nobody in the prison could remember such a good day. Chuck and the other Christians received some teasing for the prayer meeting, but by the end of the following day, Wednesday, the teasing had stopped. Everyone knew that something special had happened for on that day too the parole count was high. Even Paul Kramer, who was not due for parole for two more years, was told that his case would be heard in the spring. Tex was released that week, but Chuck, Paul and Amos decided to continue praying together every evening.

Hearing this, another man, Lee Corbin, approached Chuck. Lee believed he was beyond redemption, for he had been a con man who had posed as a preacher. He swindled dozens of people both when he was a preacher and when he was concentrating on other false business deals. He had known that what he was doing was wrong and hated himself for it, but he had become addicted to all the wealth it had brought him. The police caught up with him and arrested him when he was attending a Christian revival meeting in South Carolina. Surprisingly, he was tried on only one count of fraud and the other charges were dropped. He was sentenced to one year.

He was filled with remorse and longed to repay

all the people he had conned, though he knew he never could. Despairing now, he thought that God would never forgive him because he could not repay his victims. Chuck guided Lee through passages in the Bible which spoke of Jesus' death on behalf of sinners and his salvation and complete forgiveness. Together, he and Lee decided that Lee needed to come to God with an open heart, confess all his wrongdoing, make a new commitment to Christ and try to pay back what he could when he could. He also needed to be set free from the temptation he had fallen into before. Chuck believed that the Holy Spirit could help him.

A few nights later Lee was praying with Chuck, Paul and Amos. At Paul's suggestion, he laid all his past sins before God, asked for forgiveness and for the Holy Spirit to come into his life. Lee prayed hard and as he did so his words changed. Chuck realized that Lee was speaking in tongues, something he had heard about but never experienced before. When Lee finished he fell back exhausted. Although Chuck still did not understand what had happened, he knew that it was no act. Over the next few days he watched Lee change from a listless, depressed person to a strong man with a sense of purpose in his life. It was clearly a direct result of Lee turning back to God and asking the Holy Spirit to come into him.

Chuck and his friends began to see God at work in Maxwell in other ways. They decided that they would always say grace before eating. To Chuck's surprise other prisoners around him at the dinner table would stop eating when he prayed and bow their heads with him. Other men also began to join them in the classroom for prayer in the evenings. Soon they had a regular Bible study meeting every Monday evening, led by a local Campus Crusade worker from outside, Martin Gay, who had been brought in with the warden's permission.

One night Martin talked about the Holy Spirit. Chuck had been struggling with the theology of the Holy Spirit for a while and listened intently. Martin spoke simply: 'Ask for it and the Holy Spirit will take total control of your life,' he said. Chuck decided to take Martin at his word and shut his eyes to pray silently. 'Father, please fill me with your Spirit,' he prayed. 'Fill me so full there's room for nothing else, no hatred, no hurt, no bitterness, no exhaustion. Lift me above it all, Father.' As he prayed Chuck felt a bubbling sensation coursing through his body, then an energizing tingling all over. Joy and strength welled up inside him and he felt more alive than ever before.

Chuck still had worries and fears, though. In particular he had never forgotten the warning that Jerry had given him that someone wanted to kill him. Chuck had prayed on many occasions that he would know who it was. One day, soon after his experience at Martin Gay's meeting, he was walking towards his dormitory when he spotted two men in front of him. The two were always together and always sullen. Chuck had been told that they were ex-policemen. As Chuck followed them across the compound a voice inside him said, 'Now, Chuck.' Chuck hurried after the men and to their, and his own, surprise said, 'Did you want to talk to me?'

They stared at Chuck in astonishment. 'Go ahead and find out now', said the younger of the two. 'Ask him.'

The older one glared at Chuck. 'Do you know what happened to me?' he growled. Chuck shook his head. The man explained that he had been a Chicago police lieutenant who had been convicted of corruption after an investigation for which he blamed Chuck. More than this, he felt that he had been unfairly convicted, framed for something he had not done. 'You were the guy who ordered the Chicago investigation. It's true, isn't it?' snapped the former lieutenant, glaring at Chuck.

Chuck shook his head. He remembered the investigation which had been started by the US Justice Department, not the White House. He told his accuser so. 'If there were political reasons, they didn't come from me. I had nothing to do with it,' said Chuck. 'That's the truth,' he added. 'I know what it's like to be a political target. Believe me, I know how you feel.'

The man looked at him for a while, sizing him up. 'Yeah, I guess you do,' he said, more softly now. They talked for a while longer about the injustices in the system until the policeman said, 'I think you're levelling with me.' They shook hands and Chuck knew that the danger was over.

Not everything that happened in those days was good, however. One night two prisoners painted grafitti all over the walls of several prison buildings. The warden responded by making certain areas out of bounds after dark, further curtailing the prisoners' movements. In another incident two men had a fight and injured each other and were carted off to other prisons without even being given the chance to tell their families where they were being sent. In addition, a man with just a few months to serve escaped; when he was recaptured several years were added to his sentence.

Chuck also watched Rodriguez, a man with severe psychiatric problems, being mistreated by the system. Rodriguez, an alcoholic, had several seizures. He was sedated but got into an argument with another inmate who hit him across the head. Rodriguez, not his attacker, was punished by being put in the 'hole' – a dark, empty cell where prisoners were sent to be disciplined. He clearly needed medical help, but his pain-filled cries were ignored. Eventually, with blood pouring from his ear where the other inmate had hit him, he was carted off to Montgomery City Jail. He would get no medical help there. Chuck watched, helpless and sickened by the experience.

There were troubles for the Christian inmates too. Paul Kramer was told that, despite the decision just weeks before, he would not be eligible for parole. He would have to face another two years in prison.

Then Lee Corbin heard that his wife wanted to leave him. Lee came to Chuck in tears, not knowing what to do but longing to get home to his wife to try to save the marriage. Chuck thought that Lee should be able to get a furlough – a short time away from prison – since the prison regulations stated that one of the reasons for furloughs was 'to maintain family ties'. The prison warden did not agree, and a desperate Lee announced that there was only one thing for it – he would have to escape. Chuck was horrified. Lee had just a few months of his sentence left. If he escaped and was caught he would be given years more to serve, probably in a maximum security prison. The thought shook Lee, who had to admit that Chuck was right. The two men prayed together and Lee went to try to talk to his wife on the telephone. He later reported that she promised not to do anything before he came home.

The most worrying problem, however, was Homer. He had fallen ill towards the end of October with what seemed to be flu. He continued to get worse and was transferred to the infirmary where his temperature reached an alarming 103 degrees. Pneumonia, if not worse, was suspected. Homer was elderly and it began to sound as if he might not survive.

Chuck, Lee, Paul and Amos continued to pray together each night and asked that God would help their faith to overcome all the terrible things that were happening. God answered their prayers in a number of ways. Lee and Paul began to feel stronger in their faith, and other prisoners started coming to them for help. Homer, however, remained ill. By the beginning of November his condition was very serious and Chuck knew that he needed excellent medical care to give him a chance of recovery. He also knew that Homer was unlikely to receive that care.

There was only one thing for it – prayer. Chuck turned to Lee, Paul and Amos and asked them if they believed in Christ's power to heal. They said that they did, though Amos had some doubts. They talked it through and Chuck said that if any of them did not believe they had to say so, because they had to pray as one. In his head Chuck believed, but he was frightened inside. They agreed to think it over and meet in Homer's room later on. If anyone had doubts, he would not attend.

At nine o'clock the four of them gathered round Homer's bed. Chuck had already learned that the visiting doctor was concerned and that there was talk of allowing Homer to go home – not because he was to be freed, but because he was dying. They told Homer what they were doing and asked him to pray with them. They knelt down around him and began to pray, fervently calling on Christ to heal Homer. Chuck could feel the Holy Spirit flooding the room and, half an hour later, at the end of their prayers, he leapt into the air yelling 'Hallelujah!' The normally reserved Chuck was not known for such things. All of them believed whole-heartedly that Homer was already being healed.

Chuck awoke early the next morning and hurried to Homer's room, expecting to find him asleep at that early hour. He peeped in and his mouth dropped open. Homer was sitting up in bed, looking pale but grinning away. The fever had left him just after the four had finished praying around his bed. He had been healed! Chuck ran back to the dormitory and woke his friends. They could scarcely believe what they heard. Hospital tests later confirmed that Homer was better. The atmosphere at Maxwell also seemed lighter and happier. Chuck found himself praising God for putting him in prison.

CHAPTER THIRTEEN

Freedom

A week or two after his remarkable recovery, a strong, fit Homer Welsh walked with Chuck to the entrance to Maxwell Prison. A marshal's car stood in the driveway and Chuck was signalled to climb into it. He was being transferred back to Fort Holabird Prison in Baltimore because he was needed in Washington as a witness in the Watergate trials of his old colleagues John Ehrlichman, Bob Haldeman, John Mitchell, Robert Mardian, Gordon Strachan and Ken Parkinson. In many ways Chuck was relieved to be leaving Maxwell since he hated the prison and its oppressive atmosphere. But he was very sad to leave his friends, particularly Homer, Paul, Lee and Amos. As he turned to wave to Homer he saw tears in his friend's eyes, and a lump welled up in Chuck's own throat.

John Dean, Herb Kalmbach and Jeb Magruder were still at Fort Holabird and Chuck was glad to see them again. He learned that they were all to be kept at Holabird until after the Watergate trials, a thought that pleased him. There he could rest more and have more dignity and privacy. In the first week or so he slept for twelve hours a night, delighting in the relative peace of his own room. Being at Holabird also meant that Patty and his Christian brothers could visit him more easily. Chuck's mother was also relieved that her son had moved back to Baltimore since it meant that she could drive down from Boston to see him. Alabama had been too far for an elderly lady to travel to on her own.

Testifying at the Watergate trials was not an easy or pleasant experience. At the time of his own trial Chuck had told some news reporters, 'I've made a commitment to Christ and I really believe that the only commandment I have is to tell the truth. I will tell the truth. I am going to state cold hard facts, as best I can recall them . . . I'm not going to manufacture things to make a case. And I won't shade anything to make a point.' Chuck carried out this commitment on the witness stand (a fact that seemed to confuse the court and public alike), stating what he had known of the bugging and the cover-up, no more and no less, even when the prosecution or the defence seemed to want him to slant his version of events. It was painful to watch his former colleagues heading towards a guilty verdict. Chuck also felt a great sorrow for the whole country that government officials – himself included – should have been involved in criminal activities.

The trial was painful for the other Watergate witnesses too, in particular for Herb Kalmbach, a man whom Chuck liked enormously and whom John Dean described in his journal as 'one of the most likable men I'd ever met'. Herb had been President Nixon's personal lawyer and had become involved in the Watergate scandal rather unwittingly. John Dean's wife Maureen said of him:

Of all the figures of Watergate, Herb Kalmbach is to me one of the most tragic. . . . If someone Herb knows and believes in asks him to do something, he will assume the request is proper or else it would not have been made. And if the request comes from someone who does not wish to reveal some of the facts, Herb will not pry. He will assume that there is good and sufficient reason for his having been told only what he was told.[1]

Herb felt the weight of his prison sentence keenly. One day he broke down on the witness stand while giving evidence about John Ehrlichman. Later that evening Chuck took him to John Dean's room to try to cheer him up. In his pyjamas, dressing gown and slippers, and with bags under his eyes, Herb looked, in John's words, 'like the saddest basset hound I'd ever seen'. He and Chuck tried to reassure him that he had no need to worry or be embarrassed about crying. 'It's the most natural thing in the world,' John told him. 'All our emotions are much closer to the edge in here.' As John and Chuck looked at Herb and saw how upset he was, they both felt tears welling up in them too. Prison and the Watergate trials had made them all far more vulnerable. The old machismo that they had surrounded themselves with during the White House years had long been broken down.

The four Watergate men spent Christmas 1974 together in prison. Christmas at Holabird was a more cheerful affair than it might have been at Maxwell. On Christmas Eve the 'principals' prepared for Christmas Day: the hitman who had killed twenty-eight people baked bread, a heroin dealer oversaw the cooking of a turkey dinner for those who wanted it, and the Italian Mafia crowd cooked lasagne. They decorated a Christmas tree and hung sheets over the holes in the walls and over the tables to make the dining rooms more attractive. Chuck and John asked the prison governor for permission to attend the midnight service at a church in Baltimore, but their request was turned down. Instead, the four Watergate men held their own small service in John's room, reading from the Bible and praying for each other and their families. Chuck also prayed quietly for his friends at Maxwell. He missed them a great deal and his heart ached as he thought of them in the dehumanizing, bleak conditions of Maxwell.

Soon after Christmas there were rumours that Chuck, John, Jeb and Herb might be released. They all filed motions asking the judges for reductions of their sentences, as was standard practice, but they expected them to be rejected. However, as no news of rejection had come through, their hopes began to rise. Perhaps once the Watergate trials ended they would be released.

On 1 January 1975 Chuck was sitting quietly in his room when there was a loud knock at his door. 'Come in,' he called, and turned to see John, grinning broadly. 'They've been found guilty,' he cried. The news had just broken that John Ehrlichman, Bob Haldeman, John Mitchell and Robert Mardian had been found guilty; Ken Parkinson was acquitted. Chuck could not share

John's delight, although he understood that John had pitted his testimony against the others and had suffered a great deal in doing so. Chuck merely felt sad. These were his old colleagues; they had served together in an Administration under a President who had been forced to resign. The country was scarred and the confidence of the American people in the Government was shaken.

John, too, once the initial feelings of elation wore off, felt little joy at the guilty verdict. He had been reading Somerset Maugham's *The Summing Up* when he had heard the news. Back in his room, he picked it up again and read:

> There is not much to choose between men. They are all a hotchpotch of greatness and littleness, of virtue and vice, of nobility and baseness. Some have more strength of character, or more opportunity, and so in one direction or another give their instincts freer play, but potentially they are the same. For my part I do not think that I am any better or any worse than most people, but I know that if I set down every action in my life and every thought that has crossed my mind the world would consider me a monster of depravity.[2]

The guilty verdicts could mean one thing, however. With the trials at an end, perhaps Chuck and his friends would be freed. The four of them planned their campaign: they would get their friends to write to President Ford; they would file new motions with the judges; they would contact the

Justice Department. They were sure that they would all be set free together. Chuck also decided that he would try to trust God to set him free.

Trusting did not seem easy, however, particularly in the next few weeks. On 8 January Chuck was in Washington answering more questions about other cases when the telephone rang in the prosecutor's office. It was John Dean's lawyer who told him with obvious emotion that John had been set free. Chuck's heart began to pound – surely he was free too. Then the lawyer broke the news. Jeb and Herb were free too, but not Chuck. Judge Sirica had sentenced the others and had set them free. Judge Gesell had sentenced Chuck and he had not decided about Chuck's future. Chuck felt like crying.

That evening, back at their home in Virginia, Patty Colson watched the news on television. One item showed Jeb Magruder and his wife Gail reunited in front of their home. The picture became blurred as Patty's eyes filled with tears. She knew she should be happy for the Magruders, the Kalmbachs and the Deans, but, she wondered, why wasn't Chuck home too?

The following days were an agony of expectation. There was no word from Judge Gesell and the minutes dragged by as Chuck sat in his room. No news was followed by bad news. Fort Holabird was to be closed down and Chuck knew he might be transferred back to Maxwell. Much as he missed Paul and the others, he did not want to return to that depressing, dark prison camp where he might have to spend another two years. How too, he wondered, would Patty cope with the long journey south to

Alabama to visit him at weekends? Then, Chuck was told that he had been disbarred – forbidden to practise law – by the Virginia Supreme Court. This came as little surprise really, but Chuck had been hoping he might be let off.

Two days later Ken Adams, one of Chuck's lawyers, called the prison. Chuck hurried to the prison office, his heart beating fast. Surely this was the call to say he was free. It was not. It was something totally unexpected and it made Chuck feel sick.

His son Christian had been arrested for possessing marijuana. He was in jail, but Ken assured Chuck that they would have him out on bail very soon. Chuck was speechless, his mind and his stomach reeling. This was the last news he was expecting. Christian was only eighteen years old and had never been any worry to them. So why this? It seemed that he had bought some marijuana and planned to sell it on in the hope of raising enough money to buy a new car. Chuck knew that his own prison sentence had hurt Chris deeply, but he had not known how badly. He believed that much of the blame lay with him.

These were probably the worst days of all Chuck's time in prison, alone in Fort Holabird. Depressed and lonely, he felt that God had given up on him and his family. He was not sure how much more he or Patty could take, and Chris was constantly in his mind. His friends were doing the best they could for him, petitioning the President and visiting regularly, and Chuck was also buoyed up by the sympathetic letters from complete strangers which came flooding in to him.

It was an act of almost unprecedented generosity and love which finally turned the tables for Chuck. On 28 January Al Quie telephoned the prison and made an offer which left Chuck nearly speechless. He had heard of an old statute which, if the President permitted, would allow him to serve the rest of Chuck's prison sentence for him. 'No, no Al, you can't,' stuttered Chuck, too astonished to know what to say. Al was determined. He believed that Chuck's family needed him and he was therefore willing to give up his own freedom for Chuck.

At first Chuck wondered if Al was out of his mind. Al had so much to lose by going into prison. He was one of the most respected politicians in Washington and held a number of senior, responsible positions. A spell in prison could ruin his career, quite apart from any problems he might have coping with the conditions. Chuck would wish prison on nobody. What he did not find out for a long time was that, ever since a visit to a prison when he was a child, Al had had a deep fear of imprisonment. He still had that fear, even when he made his offer to Chuck. Chuck knew that Al was deadly serious. Equally serious, Chuck turned down his offer.

The next day Doug wrote to him, telling him that not just Al but he, Harold and Graham would offer to serve the rest of Chuck's sentence. Doug believed that Chuck had an important role to play in the US in the future, using his undoubted gifts to help his fellow countrymen and women find peace and better lives. He wrote, 'If I could, I would gladly give my life so you could use the wonderful gifts of

God, that he has entrusted you with, to the glory of God.'

Looking back, Chuck wrote:

It was almost more than I imagined possible, this love of one man for another. Christ's love. Al Quie would give up his whole career, Doug Coe would lay down his life, Graham and Harold, too. Isn't that what it's really all about? Isn't that the overwhelming gain of knowing Christ Jesus which makes all else as 'loss'? And this day I knew him as never before. I'd felt his presence all right, but now I knew his power and love through the deep caring of four men. All the pain and agony to mind and body was small in comparison.[3]

That evening Chuck surrendered everything to God, praising him for what had happened, even for Chris's arrest. As he did so he felt an enormous joy and freedom.

On Friday 31 January 1975, just after five in the afternoon, Dave Shapiro telephoned the prison. Chuck was once again summoned to the prison office. Tentatively he picked up the receiver. 'You're free!' shouted Dave.

Notes

1 Maureen Dean with Hays Goney, *Mo: A Woman's View of Watergate*, New York, Simon and Schuster, 1975.
2 Somerset Maugham, *The Summing Up*, London, William Heineman, 1938.
3 Charles Colson, *Born Again*, London, Hodder & Stoughton, 1979.

CHAPTER FOURTEEN

An Uncertain Future

'Oh, Chuck!' Patty flung her arms around Chuck and hugged him tightly. Behind them they could hear cheers and calls of goodbye. A group of Mafia men, con artists, hitmen, drugs traffickers and other criminals were waving from the prison. Slowly it sunk in: he was free!

Everything around him seemed bright, fresh and clean, even though it was a dark winter's night and the sky was heavy with the smoke from the Baltimore factories. Chuck had never thought that a car could be as lovely as his and Patty's red station wagon seemed when they drove off.

'Life will be different from now on,' thought Chuck. 'I'll be able to spend more time with Patty and the children.' Chuck felt that he had spent too little time with his family over the past few years. If he had had more time, he thought, perhaps Chris would not have got into trouble.

Chuck was not sure exactly what he wanted to do next, but he had had enough of life in the spotlight. 'Perhaps,' he thought, 'I can find a job in business, something challenging but which leaves me enough time for myself and the family.' He longed to go for long walks in the countryside, travel, enjoy all the little things that he used to take for granted before going to prison – fresh air, flowers, birds, trees, and above all, peace.

There was little chance of peace as Patty turned the car into their drive. Dozens of reporters were huddled together, shivering in the cold night air, microphones and cameras at the ready to interview Chuck about his future. Questions came at him from all sides as he and Patty pushed through to the front door. Chuck turned and made a brief statement, thanking both Judge Gesell and God that he was free. The next day he smiled when he picked up the newspaper and saw the headline 'Gesell frees Colson; Colson thanks the Lord'.

It should have been bliss to lie in his own bed that night with Patty beside him, thinking quietly of what he would do now that he was free. Strangely, however, Chuck did not feel at all peaceful, and when he finally fell asleep he had a nightmare. Suddenly he was back in the stifling atmosphere of the dormitory at Maxwell, listening to the groans of other men around him, men who felt desperate at their fate. He awoke with a start, disoriented and frightened, and he lay awake long afterwards, thinking of the men he had left behind. He had cared for them when he had been in prison and he cared about them now, but what could he do to help?

Chuck and Patty had a more immediate problem to sort out – Chuck's son Chris who was in Columbia, South Carolina. Chris's drugs charge was one of the reasons that Judge Gesell had decided to set Chuck free. They flew to Columbia and when they met Chris at the airport any thoughts of being stern were immediately forgotten. He was visibly shaken by his experience and all Chuck could do was hug him and tell him that they would support him. The charges were later dropped.

From Columbia, Chuck and Patty took the short flight to Alabama and Maxwell Prison to visit Paul Kramer. As they drove through the gates towards the prison Chuck felt some of the old sensations of fear and claustrophobia returning to him. He was a visitor now, but the memories of his weeks in Maxwell were horribly vivid. However when they arrived and he saw Paul running towards him across the compound, Chuck's feelings turned to joy and delight. Without thinking he opened his arms and gave Paul a huge hug.

The incident was recorded on film, since news of Chuck's visit had leaked out to the press and a camera team and reporters turned up at Maxwell in the hope of a story. Noticing them, Chuck worried that the hug might have been misconstrued and that the news story might be one suggesting that he and Paul were homosexual, since homosexual relationships are common in prisons. Several weeks later, however, he learned that the incident had had a rather different effect. One man who wrote to him said, 'Seeing a once-powerful White House official embracing that poor prisoner got to me somehow as none of the other arguments ever did. I knew Christianity had to be real.'

Over the weeks that followed memories of Maxwell haunted Chuck and he frequently suffered nightmares about the men there. During the day he was often listless and short-tempered, which was not what he was expecting at all. He had no real idea what he wanted to do and hated the inactivity. 'Chuck,' said Sylvia Mary Alison, who set up Prison Fellowship in England, 'is like a dynamo always needing to churn something around, and he finds it very hard if he doesn't have a clear focus.'

Chuck felt torn in many directions. He could not practise law in Virginia, though the Massachusetts State Bar had only suspended him so there was hope that he would be able to practise again there. Patty in particular hoped so. Doug and the other brothers wanted him to do work for projects connected with Fellowship House, the Christian centre in Washington where they met regularly for prayer, Bible study and fellowship. Others, including Richard Nixon, advised him to go into business. Then there was prison work. Much as he longed to help Paul and other prisoners, he felt that he could not bear to go back inside a prison. Perhaps he could help with reform from the outside by talking and writing about it, persuading old friends in positions of power to urge reform.

He did not want to go on lecture tours since there had been a great deal of criticism of other Watergate figures making a lot of money out of speaking about their experiences. Chuck had, in fact, promised Judge Gesell that he would not do the same. If he spoke at the occasional prayer breakfast or Christian meeting he would give any speaking fees to a fund set up for work in prisons.

Above all, Chuck wanted to know what God wanted him to do with his life. Patty, too, was worried about the future. She dreaded him returning to public life, and Chuck wished he could reassure her.

In the meantime, there was one immediate task to finish. In prison he had started to write the story of his conversion and this was turning into a full-length book. Chuck was offered money by several publishers for the story of his life, but he felt that many of them would expect a book full of criticisms of Richard Nixon. He was not prepared to go along with that. He was therefore pleased when a Christian publisher, Chosen Books, offered him a small advance for the type of book he wanted to write. The result was his autobiography *Born Again*, which became a bestseller and was later made into a film.

While he was writing *Born Again* Chuck had little time for day-to-day administrative tasks such as replying to invitations to speak at events. He therefore asked an old and respected friend, Fred Rhodes, to join him as his business partner. Fred had held a number of responsible government positions but had taken early retirement. While Chuck was still in prison he had written, offering to help him in any way once he was released.

Fred's constant questions about prison life and Chuck's fellow prisoners made Chuck face up to the challenge that he should do something to help prisoners. Harold Hughes also challenged him to take action, rather than just complaining – as Chuck frequently did – about the prison system and its injustices. As winter turned to spring Chuck knew he had to make a decision.

The Plan Unfolds

In the end, Chuck's decision came remarkably easily. It simply appeared in his mind one sunny Saturday morning in April 1975. He had clambered sleepily out of bed, thinking of nothing more than whether spring had arrived yet. Peering at his face, he began to shave slowly in front of the mirror. Suddenly he was wide awake as a series of images flashed across his mind. He could picture men and women wearing prison garments coming out of prisons, sitting in classrooms, holding discussions and Bible studies, praying. 'Of course,' he muttered. 'Take the prisoners out, teach them and return them to prisons to build Christian fellowships. Spread these fellowships through every penitentiary in America.'

He was wide awake now as he saw the plan unfolding before him. It did not seem to be a plan *he* had thought up, but something that he was being told about and was responding to. Not sure whether it was coming from God or whether it was just his own flash of human inspiration, he quickly finished shaving and rushed to the telephone to call Harold.

Twenty minutes later Harold reached the house and settled down to hear the plan which was becoming clearer in Chuck's mind as he spoke. 'Two prisoners from each of a number of prisons could come out on furlough for, say, two weeks at a time. They could be put up somewhere near Fellowship House and then attend seminars about Christian living and the Bible in Fellowship House itself,' he said excitedly. Chuck was convinced that the only way to make a real difference to prisons and prisoners was through Jesus Christ.

Harold nodded. He was sure from what Chuck had told him that the inspiration had come from God, but he expressed doubts that they would ever get permission to get such a scheme started. He had been involved in prison reform years ago when he was Governor of Iowa, and he had met opposition and problems at every step of the way. That was in just one State, and Chuck was talking about a programe to cover the whole of the USA.

They prayed hard about it and decided to start at the top by arranging a meeting with Senator James Eastland, Chairman of the Judiciary Committee (which deals with all laws relating to criminal justice and prisons). He was a powerful man who could get things done and was also a good friend of Harold's. The senator was sympathetic, nodding with interest as they talked, and at the end of the two-hour meeting he said that he would try to do something to help.

Such work in prisons was, however, low on the list of the Judiciary Committee's priorities. Chuck and Harold spent a frustrating few weeks waiting for news from Senator Eastland's office, calling occasionally only to be told that their request was being considered. Elsewhere they met the same type of response. Old political colleagues agreed that it was a 'nice idea' to help prisoners, but they were not sufficiently interested to do anything much about it. Chuck hated this waiting and by June had had enough.

Eager for action he suggested to Harold that they might try contacting Norman Carlson, head of the Bureau of Prisons. Chuck was not really hopeful that he would agree to their plans, since people in government did not usually relish the thought of giving prisoners furloughs. They tried a slightly unusual tack. When Carlson's secretary asked what they wanted to meet him about they replied, 'It's about bringing Jesus Christ into prisons.' Their appointment was booked for the following day.

Norman Carlson was a straightforward man, so well respected that three years earlier he had received an award for being one of the ten out-standing people in government service. He greeted them warmly and listened while Chuck spoke of his own experiences, both of being in prison and of how Jesus Christ had transformed his life. He then outlined their plans – tentatively at first, since he knew that they might offend Carlson. Much of what he said seemed to criticize the Bureau of Prisons: that prisons are terrible holes; that they don't rehabilitate; that the Government and taxpayers are spending billions on prisoners, and yet, according to one survey, four out of five crimes are committed by ex-convicts. Carlson listened in silence, his face betraying nothing. 'Mr Carlson,' said Chuck at last, 'the prisons – your prisons – aren't helping these men. Everybody there, even the best of your staff, are looked upon as cops. But one Person can make a difference: Jesus Christ. His love and power to remake lives is the answer. He will heal and reconcile. I know it. I saw it happen. Give us a chance to prove it.'

Carlson still said nothing. Chuck was sure that he was going to be shown the door, particularly when he asked Carlson to issue an order allowing them to go into any federal prison in the USA and select prisoners for training. Then Carlson spoke. 'A few weeks ago,' he said, 'my wife and I were at the Terminal Island Prison in southern California. On Sunday we went to chapel. At one point in the service the chaplain asked the inmates to join in with spontaneous prayers. In the back – I couldn't see him – a man prayed for my wife and me. I was surprised that he did that.'

Chuck and Harold hardly knew what to say, except that Christians were taught to pray for those in authority. This did not satisfy Carlson who was puzzled why anyone should pray for the man who was effectively his captor. Chuck looked at him intently and replied, 'That man prayed for you because he loves you.'

Carlson simply shook his head, clearly bemused, however a few minutes later he agreed to their plans and promised to issue the appropriate orders. It was Chuck's turn to be bemused, although his bewilderment was mixed with joy. It did not occur to him at the time that the prayer of an unknown prisoner in the chapel at Terminal Island Prison could have the power to persuade Carlson to give Christianity a chance in prisons.

Unfortunately, the next steps were not so straightforward. The first training session was planned for November in Fellowship House. Fellowship House is in an attractive, affluent residential area and when word leaked out that Chuck and Harold were planning to bring prisoners to the neighbourhood, the local residents were up in arms. Imagining that there would soon be dangerous, violent criminals prowling the streets looking for innocent victims, they set up a neighbourhood association to fight Chuck and Harold, even going as far as threatening court action. Doug Coe spent a long time with angry residents persuading them that they would not be endangered and that property prices were unlikely to fall as a result of the training sessions.

Meanwhile Fred Rhodes invited Christians from around the USA who had high profiles in business and the professions to come to Washington to learn about prison visiting. They then went into prisons near their homes to interview Christian prisoners and recommend which ones should attend. This did not always please the prison chaplains, some of whom felt that they should be able to select the prisoners. But Chuck believed that they would not gain the trust of prisoners if government-appointed chaplains were involved. Prison warders had the final say about whether or not they could have furloughs.

While all this was going on Chuck was having his own problems. First, he was coming up against opposition when he turned down invitations to speak at Christian meetings. Mindful of his promise to Judge Gesell and his wish to steer clear of the limelight, he did not want to carry out public speaking engagements. Eventually, however, he felt that he was doing more harm than good by refusing, so he agreed to a few, making it clear that his fees were to be given to the work of prison reform. There were occasions, however, much to Chuck's astonishment and disgust, when people forgot or did not bother to send on the money that had been agreed. He had not expected Christians to behave like that, but he was learning.

Meanwhile, painful memories of Watergate accusations were being stirred up for Chuck. In September 1975 an article appeared in the *Washington Post* claiming that a senior official in the White House had ordered Howard Hunt to kill newspaper columnist Jack Anderson, a frequent critic of the Nixon Administration. The article inferred that Chuck had approved the plan. Immediately other newspapers, hungry for a good story, joined in. Soon it seemed that Chuck might have to face a grand jury who would decide whether he would stand trial for attempted murder.

Chuck reeled from the shock. He had certainly known of no such plan and could not believe that anyone in the White House would be either so wicked or so stupid as to want to kill Jack Anderson, however much he criticized the Government. With Doug, Harold, Al and Graham's support and encouragement, Chuck offered the false accusations to God. Yet it was a struggle for him and a terrifying experience to be linked with an alleged murder plot, however unlikely it was. Eventually the accusations died down.

Slowly, despite the setbacks and other personal

griefs, Chuck inched towards the first training session for prisoners, scheduled to start on Sunday 2 November 1975. It had seemed so simple when the idea first appeared in Chuck's mind, but now he was assailed by doubts. How would the prisoners react to being free for those two weeks? Would there be any trouble? The continuation of the project rested to a large extent on the success of this first session.

The prisoners were chosen from six prisons in four different States. Ten men and two women, six black and six white, were expected at the Good News Mission – where they would sleep – at seven on Sunday evening. They would have no guards with them during the drive or for any time in the following two weeks. By seven o'clock, ten prisoners had arrived but two were missing. Chuck was on edge. Surely nothing could have gone wrong so early? He need not have worried. Three-quarters of an hour later the two men arrived: their driver had taken a wrong turn.

After dinner Chuck said a few words to welcome the prisoners. The twelve listened courteously, but their attention was really caught when Harold started talking in his strong, deep voice. He spoke of their task there: 'to learn what it means to be disciples who deny everything else in the world for the sake of Jesus Christ'. He also demonstrated his empathy with them, telling them, 'I know what it's like to be a prisoner. I was thrown in jail in six States when I was an alcoholic and should have been in twenty. Chuck has been there too. We're no better than you, but we are going to teach you.'

The next two weeks were a real joy. Fred Rhodes drove the trainees to Fellowship House each day where they worked hard, listening attentively to talks on Jesus, the Christian life, fellowship and the Bible. They studied their Bibles eagerly, and the only rule they broke was to stay up later than they had been asked to because they wanted to carry on praying and singing hymns.

There was one man who made a particular impression on Chuck that week. He was a tall, strong, black man nicknamed Soul. At first Chuck was nervous about him, since he knew Soul had spent the past seven years in Lewisburg Penitentiary in Pennsylvania on a charge of armed robbery. He had almost another eighteen years to serve. Chuck could not help wondering how he would cope with these two weeks of freedom, away from the grey, thirty-five-foot wall which was a Lewisburg prisoner's only outlook.

If Chuck had any worries, they were completely dissolved by the end of the first week. On the Sunday after church the trainees were given a free day and allowed to choose where they wanted to go. Soul came up to the leaders and announced that they would like to visit Arlington County Jail to talk to the men there. Far from wanting to escape, they decided to go back inside a prison.

The inmates of Arlington County Jail appreciated the visit, chatting easily to Soul and the others. Then Soul asked to visit the maximum security unit. Here, it seemed, he was less welcome. Most of the men in the unit were black and Soul arrived there with two white men – Bill Simmer, who ran the Good News

Mission, and a deputy sheriff. Seeing the white officials, and Soul in a smart suit, some of the inmates called out abuse, telling Soul he was a traitor. Soul took no notice, waiting patiently while the door to the prison cell was unlocked. The jeers stopped and the prisoners watched in astonishment as Soul walked in. He spent the next half hour talking to a small group of prisoners while Bill Simmer and the deputy sheriff waited anxiously outside. Eventually they heard someone crying. Soul walked over to the door, his arms around two men, both of whom were in tears. With a huge smile on his face, Soul announced that these two men had turned to Jesus.

There were other victories and joys in that fortnight. The tension with the local residents around Fellowship House had never quite resolved itself and Chuck waited daily for a court order to stop the programme. One day Chuck and the others invited the locals to lunch at Fellowship House. The prisoners attended, dressed in ordinary clothes, along with other men and women who used Fellowship House regularly. After a while Chuck asked some of the local residents to pick out the prisoners among the luncheon guests. Most could not do it. They chatted amicably with the prisoners and after that day there were no more complaints, and certainly no threat of court action.

That first training fortnight was a high point for everyone involved. At the end they held a communion service, attended by over 200 people including the spouses of most of the prisoners and some local residents. The next day the inmates returned to their prisons, some of them with many years of their sentences still to go before they could taste freedom again. Yet they were far from discouraged by the thought. As they piled into the cars for the journey back to captivity, one of them turned and said, 'I do not go back as a prisoner but as a disciple on a commission for Jesus Christ.'

The following year reports came in from the jails where the inmates had returned. Some had encountered opposition but were working away all the same. Others had had a better reception. Lewisburg Penitentiary, where Soul was incarcerated, was one of the toughest, roughest prisons in the US, where violence and murder were commonplace. Now a small miracle was taking place, with prisoners and guards alike committing their lives to Christ.

More good news arrived early in 1976. Buoyed up by the success of the first training session, Chuck and his Fellowship House colleagues began planning the next. They were still debating who should lead it when Chuck received a telephone call. It was from Paul Kramer in Maxwell Prison. Paul was coming to the end of his sentence and Fellowship House had offered to take care of him if he were given probation for the last three months. To Paul's delight his probation had been agreed. Chuck was delighted too. Not only was a dear friend to be released, they also had the perfect leader for the next training session.

Paul's release came a week earlier than he had anticipated. As soon as he was given his release date, he wrote to Chuck and Patty telling them that he would take the bus from Montgomery, Alabama, to Washington. The bus trip took twenty-four hours. On a cold, blustery Saturday afternoon Paul arrived at Washington central bus terminal, stiff and tired after his journey and nervously excited at the thought of his new life ahead. Clutching a small duffel bag with his few possessions inside and just $25 in his pocket, he ran down the steps from the bus expecting to see Chuck or Patty waving to him. They were nowhere in sight.

Paul was not too worried at first: he assumed they had been held up in traffic. But as the minutes ticked by he began to think that something was seriously wrong. The bus station was draughty, cold and dirty and smelled rather like the prison Paul had left behind the day before. A few drunks slumped down on benches nearby and Paul could see nobody who looked as if they might help him. He found a telephone box and dialled Chuck and Patty. There was no reply. Then he telephoned Fellowship House. They knew nothing about him. Finally, almost desperate now, he remembered that Chuck had mentioned in a letter a place called the Good News Mission in nearby Arlington. He fished the letter out of his duffel bag and checked for an address. He thanked God that Chuck had thought to give it. Paul flagged down a taxi cab and, praying fervently that he would be welcomed, he set out for Arlington.

At the Good News Mission Bill Simmer greeted him warmly and offered him a bed. He later discovered that Chuck and Patty, not expecting him to be freed so soon, had left Washington for a few days without seeing his letter. Two days later Chuck and Patty returned and were upset when they discovered what had happened. The experience underlined for them the need to ensure that ex-prisoners are welcomed back into the community.

Paul agreed to take charge of the second training session, but he also wanted to know what he would be doing after that. Like so many former prisoners, his previous life had been in ruins and he needed to make sure he had plans for the future. Chuck wanted to reassure him, but he did not even know himself what he was planning to do full-time. He knew, however, that it was time that he found out.

CHAPTER SIXTEEN

Teething Troubles

The plans for the second training session were revealing some weaknesses. While Chuck's plans for prison work were national in scale, others thought more locally. A former District of Columbia government official, John Staggers, had provided a great deal of help and support during the first session. He had administered a prison-visiting and welfare programme for a few years at Lorton Penitentiary, south of Washington, and as a result of his dedicated guidance a small Christian fellowship group had started up. It had grown steadily and the prison benefited as the level of violence began to fall.

Chuck planned the second session for the last two weeks of February 1976 and he asked John Staggers to keep that period free. Without realizing it Chuck was showing signs of slipping back into his old ways, forgetting to consult people before telling them what they had to do. John, with his wealth of experience in the local prison, wanted to plan the next session with Chuck; while Chuck was ready to race ahead, merely telling John what was expected of him. John had seen how successful the last session had been, but was not sure whether the same success could be repeated month after month. He knew how long it had taken to build up a fellowship in just one prison and was not convinced that Chuck's large-scale plans could work.

John provided a wise word of caution. Also, the team realized that they had not fully worked out exactly what they were trying to accomplish. However they agreed to continue with the next session and then to act more cautiously. All the time Chuck was discovering that he had a lot to learn about prison work.

If Chuck felt disappointed at the tensions between him and John Staggers, he was further disheartened by what was to come. Some of the group of prisoners to arrive for the second training session were less dedicated and mature than those at the first session. One of the two women, Jennifer, was particularly difficult. A former model who had become mixed up in drugs, she was an attractive, young blonde. On the first evening she turned up in a see-through blouse and no bra. She was quite aware of the temptation that she posed to sex-starved prisoners and was happy to tempt. She told Fred Rhodes, who tried to talk to her, that she could take care of herself and that if any man did try to force himself on her she might rather enjoy it. Fred sadly told her of her duty to obey Christ, and warned her that she would go back to prison if there was any trouble.

Fortunately, the other female inmate and a female Fellowship House volunteer kept a close watch on Jennifer, even choosing the clothes she should wear each day and sometimes literally forcing her to wear them. As a result of their watchfulness, and a great deal of prayer, the fortnight passed without too much incident.

Another prisoner was found to be taking drugs, although he did respond to a firm warning and settled down later on. Other prisoners, too, violated some of the rules. By the end of the two weeks Chuck, Paul and the other organizers were exhausted and relieved it was over. There had been some positive experiences, and one inmate in particular demonstrated a mature faith, but on the whole the session had not been a success.

They knew that before they went any further they would have to make changes. For a start, they would have no more mixed-sex classes. They also realized that they had not planned properly and that even the teaching was not always thoroughly prepared. Above all, however, they were aware that they were not united in their purpose. This fundamental problem was holding them all back.

During the eighteen months or so after his release from prison Chuck learned a great deal about the Christian life. It was certainly more difficult than some Christians lead others to believe. Christian biographies and books about Christian living frequently suggest that once Jesus has come into someone's life, victory follows victory, joy piles upon joy. What is not mentioned so often is that there are plenty of setbacks too. Chuck was slowly learning this. First there was the tension between him and John Staggers, next there was the second training session. Sometimes, too, visits to prisons were discouraging.

One particularly disheartening visit took place in the early spring of 1976. Chuck had arranged to visit Minneapolis-St Paul, Minnesota, to talk to a number of Christian groups there. In return, a group of Christian business people had promised to raise $5,000 for the work in prisons. The meetings were scheduled over two and a half days, with a final afternoon being left free for Chuck to visit Sandstone Federal Penitentiary, some ninety miles north of Minneapolis. He hoped that he might find some prisoners there who could come to the Washington training sessions.

The prison work desperately needed money if it was to survive. Chuck's heart sank when, towards the end of his stay in Minneapolis, he learned that only $3,400 of the expected $5,000 had been raised. If Chuck was depressed by this, he became more depressed by his visit to Sandstone. He flew there with a local Christian pilot Dave Rolschau. Set far out in the cold Minnesota countryside, Sandstone had an atmosphere of bleak isolation.

There was clearly little in the way of Christian fellowship there, though the prison chaplain struggled on with chapel every week. Chuck thought that if they visited the dormitories some Christians might come forward, so he and Dave were escorted through one housing unit after another. Dave was stunned by the conditions – the cold, the double-decked bunk beds, the blankets hung over the windows to lessen the icy draughts, and above all the hopeless atmosphere. Chuck, more used to it, was less shocked, but he was deeply disappointed that no one approached them. A few nodded at them, a few turned their backs, and some of them laughed scornfully when Chuck mentioned Bible studies. Out of the 500 inmates at Sandstone, not one Christian came forward that day.

Chuck and Dave left feeling rather depressed, and even the chaplain seemed relieved to see them go. Before they took off, however, Chuck suggested to Dave that they should pray together. With the engine ticking over, they bowed their heads and Chuck prayed: 'Lord, we may be a couple of fools, but we claim this place for you. It's impossible, I know, so if you want us here, you'll have to do it.'

One positive result of Chuck's few days in Minnesota emerged soon after. He had been back in Washington for only a week or so when a cheque for $1,000 arrived from a man who had sat next to him at a dinner in Minneapolis-St Paul. Other cheques for smaller amounts followed and the total raised by the Minnesota trip was eventually $5,100 – $100 over the target.

Back in Washington the prison work seemed to be slowing down. Some chaplains and wardens were expressing disapproval of Chuck's prison work. Things were not helped when Slim, one of their second group of trainee prisoners, escaped from his maximum security prison in Atlanta soon after returning from Washington. Chuck could not understand why Slim should wait until he was back in prison to make his escape bid when he could have just walked away while he was in Washington. Whatever the reason, the incident did little to improve relations with the prison system. They later discovered that Slim's life had been threatened and he believed that this was the only way of saving it.

Tensions also continued between Chuck and John Staggers, and eventually Chuck offered to hand over the leadership of the project to him. Prison work was only taking up part of Chuck's time; perhaps he might be better off in business or practising law in Massachusetts, and acting as a fundraiser for the ministry instead. John turned down the offer, but Chuck's willingness to relinquish control eased some of the tension and they proceeded with a third training fortnight.

This one was much more successful, helped in part by the presence of George Soltau, a Reformed Presbyterian minister from Dallas, Texas. George had a background in prison ministry and brought great professionalism to the teaching. His prison experience had also instilled in him the importance of restoring a prisoner's sense of self-worth, teaching him or her that one's sins can be forgiven. Without this, a criminal often sees little worth in others and continues in crime. As a result of George's insights, they included several lessons in the training sessions about the characteristics of God and how humans are made in God's image.

Meanwhile, Chuck's autobiography *Born Again* was published and became an immediate success. Fred accompanied Chuck as he toured the country, appearing on television programmes and attending book-signing sessions. The royalties soon began to pour in and eased the financial pressure on the prison work. Chuck also received letters from readers across the US and even further afield, many of them telling how his story had helped them in their own lives.

Chuck was also being drawn more and more into evangelistic work, speaking at meetings and encouraging his listeners to come forward at the end to accept Jesus into their lives. In the summer of 1976 *Born Again* was to be published in Europe. Chuck was invited to make a tour of the Continent to give television appearances, speak at press conferences and address some Christian meetings. Sometimes Chuck wondered whether God wanted him to be a full-time evangelist.

Patty was not so sure. Although she wanted to support Chuck in whatever he did, she felt uncertain about what was happening in their lives. Chuck knew this and decided to set himself a deadline. He and Patty would spend a month in Europe, starting in early June. Chuck determined that by 1 August 1976 he would make up his mind about his future career.

The trip to Europe was a sobering experience for Chuck. The Church is strong in the USA, and at the time of Chuck's European visit it was growing steadily. In Europe the situation was very different. Chuck travelled to Belgium where he was told by one man that there were probably only 1,000 real Christians in a country of ten million people. Chuck was not sure whether his source was painting too gloomy a picture, but certainly he did not encounter anything like the enthusiastic interest in Christianity which he was used to on the other side of the Atlantic.

Elsewhere the story was also depressing. In the course of six days Chuck visited six countries – Belgium, Germany, Holland, Denmark, Sweden and Finland – before flying to the United Kingdom to join Patty and his daughter Emily, who were holidaying there. Across Europe Chuck met a number of strong, faithful Christians, but the message was always the same: they were battling against agnosticism, secularism and indifference. Chuck realized how lucky he was to be surrounded by Christians back home.

His trip to Europe impressed Chuck in more ways than one. He was shocked that there seemed to be so few Christians ready to stand up and be counted, but he was deeply moved by a constant characteristic in the ones he met – obedience to Christ. Over the days that followed, as Chuck approached the 1 August deadline that he had set himself, this fact weighed heavily on his mind. Obedience seemed the key to his future.

One summer's night in July 1976, when they were back in Washington, Chuck sat up late. Patty had gone to bed and the house was quiet. He took up a yellow legal notepad, just like the one he had used to outline the pros and cons for believing the Christian Gospel three years before, and began to jot down what had happened to him since becoming a Christian. Over those three years Chuck's life had been transformed, but during most of that time he had relied on experience and feelings – emotions in the heart. Later, in his second book *Life Sentence*, Chuck wrote: 'It is understandable that sins of the heart, such as temper, hatred, jealousy and pride, are the first to be affected in one's conversion. But it is only the beginning, only one part of the transforming process God intends for our lives. If we are to be new creations, much more is demanded: heart, body, spirit and mind.'[1]

He then recalled a verse from the Bible, when St Paul, writing to the Romans, said, 'Do not be conformed to this world, but be transformed by the renewal of your mind, that you may prove what is the will of God, that which is good and acceptable, and perfect.' (Romans 12:2) 'That,' said Chuck to himself, 'is the key. I have to make a break with the past that is so radical that I fill my mind with the thoughts of Christ.'

It seemed a daunting prospect, but he believed that God was asking him to think about what it really meant to live as Christ's disciple. The more he pondered this, the more it seemed to be linked with obedience to Christ, the same sort of obedience that he had witnessed among the Christians in Europe. As the hours ticked by and the sky became lighter Chuck reached a decision. Deep in his heart he knew that obedience to Christ meant one thing for him – that his future work should be a full-time ministry to prisons.

Chuck felt enormous relief: now he was certain of the path he had to take. There was only one thing that held him back – he did not think that Patty would be happy. Chuck, however, underestimated his wife. Patty had watched Chuck over the preceding months and realized that he was happiest doing prison work. Though her inclination was for a quiet life out of the limelight, she believed firmly that God wanted Chuck to work in prisons and she was therefore prepared to support him.

One night late that summer, while they were spending a few days on the west coast of the USA in Oregon, she told Chuck of her decision: she would

146

always be there for him in his work. Chuck leapt out of his chair and grabbed hold of her, hugging her tightly. He knew what an enormous sacrifice she was making. 'So where do we go next, Chuck Colson?' she asked.

'Into the prisons, Honey. Into every prison in this country.'

'They will never be the same if you do.'

'I pray to God that you are right – that he will see to it that they never are the same again.'

Note

1 Charles Colson, *Life Sentence*, London, Hodder and Stoughton, 1978.

CHAPTER SEVENTEEN

The Presence of God

'Right, we need an office, a secretary, some staff – preferably an ex-prisoner or two,' said Chuck. He and Patty had been joined in Oregon by Fred Rhodes and his wife, and Chuck and Fred were talking about the future of the prison ministry now that Chuck had decided to go full-time. Chuck was excited, but worried about all the paperwork that setting up a ministry would involve. Fred, however, calmly produced a folder full of forms. He had thought Chuck would come to the decision to go into full-time prison ministry and had come prepared.

Back home, they hired a two-roomed office for $350 a month in Arlington, just a few miles outside of Washington. Within a week they had it furnished with desks made by Chuck's son Wendell and surplus filing cabinets and typewriters which Fred provided. Paul Kramer was soon installed, as was Jackie Butner, a former prisoner who had attended the second training session. Jackie was a former bank clerk so she took charge of the accounts. Fred became President of the new company and Gordon Loux, whom Chuck had met at a Christian book-sellers'convention the previous year, was invited to manage the daily running of the office. Other volunteers came forward to help and soon the office was buzzing with activity. The name of the new ministry came easily to them: Prison Fellowship; and the training sessions were renamed Washington Discipleship Seminars.

Another discipleship seminar had been fixed for mid-August and this was a particular success. Among the prisoners attending was Tommy Tarrants, a former member of the White Knights, the most violent branch of the Ku Klux Klan: a viciously racist group which uses terrorism and violence against non-whites. Tommy had been imprisoned in the late 1960s but had undergone a tremendous conversion. He was now a model prisoner and, during his two weeks at Fellowship House, was a very studious member of the group. He was not, however, expecting to meet a man who, in his White Knights days, he hated above almost any other. That man was Eldridge Cleaver, former leader of the radical Black Panther movement which used violence in its campaign for equal rights for black men and women.

Eldridge had voluntarily returned to the US the previous year to stand trial for his part in a shooting, back in 1968. He had become a Christian and had been bailed out of prison in Oregon. Now he was to appear on a television programme called *Meet the Press*, and was brought to Fellowship House to talk to Chuck about how to deal with the media. Chuck himself found it difficult enough to meet him. As a staunch Republican, Chuck found militant radicals extremely hard to deal with. But for Tommy and Eldridge the meeting was especially difficult and humbling. The power of their experience of Jesus

Christ carried them through it. Eldridge took Tommy's hand in his firm grip and said, looking straight into his eyes, 'We both have a lot to live down, don't we?' It was moments like this that reinforced Chuck in his faith, both in Jesus Christ and in the prison ministry.

Other times were less encouraging. Lee Corbin, Chuck and Paul's old friend from Maxwell, was out of prison on parole. Chuck contacted him to ask him if he needed any help, but Lee insisted that he was doing fine. Lee called from time to time and told Chuck that he had found part-time work and was managing all right for money. Chuck took him at his word. Then, one afternoon, Paul came to see Chuck with the dreadful news: Lee was back in prison. Lee, it seemed, had slipped back into his old ways of petty swindling and fraud. It was likely that he would be given a further sentence of five years, unless Chuck went to plead for him.

Lee's parole hearing was in Aiken, South Carolina the following week. Chuck's heart went out to Lee as he saw him being led into the courtroom. He realized that it was he who had failed his friend, not the other way around. When Lee had telephoned from time to time, Chuck felt that he should have realized that he had been sending coded messages asking for support and encouragement. But Chuck had been deaf to them. Chuck may have offered him money, but it was fellowship that he really needed.

As the clerk read out the list of Lee's crimes – obtaining fraudulent credit, failing to pay what he owed, petty swindling – it seemed that all was lost. Lee would be back inside for five years. Finally, the lawyer asked the judge to hear Chuck's plea. Chuck stood up in the witness stand and gave it his all. He placed the blame on himself, for failing to support a man in need, and asked that Lee should be given another chance. The judge seemed unimpressed, then brought out a copy of *Born Again*. He read from it extracts in which Chuck had talked about Lee and his previous failings, even mentioning the time that Lee had wanted to escape from Maxwell. It clearly did not help his case.

Lee pleaded guilty and they waited for the fall of the gavel. A long time seemed to pass while the judge considered his sentence. It seemed that Chuck's plea had helped after all. The judge gave Lee a fifteen-month sentence.

Lee turned to Chuck, tears in his eyes, and Chuck rushed forward to hug him and to ask for forgiveness. Lee assured him there was nothing to forgive; he was just overwhelmingly grateful to Chuck for his help. Chuck watched as Lee was led away in handcuffs.

This experience was a lesson that Chuck never forgot. He wrote later: 'Grandiose schemes for the cure of prison ills all across America wouldn't be worth a thing if they blinded me to my commitment to care for one person in need.'[1]

The Prison Fellowship schemes, though not 'grandiose' at the time, were, however, to become larger. Prison chaplains were beginning to believe that the Fellowship House work was a dynamic way of transforming the religious life of prisons. In January 1977 Norman Carlson, head of the Bureau of Prisons, asked Chuck if Fellowship House could provide a chaplain for a new prison in Memphis. Chuck agreed immediately. It was an opportunity not to be missed.

Two days later the 1977 National Prayer Breakfast took place. A seminar on Prison Fellowship was scheduled for the afternoon, and as Chuck sat listening to some of the former prisoners giving their testimony to a rapt audience he felt a growing conviction that the right man to become the Memphis chaplain was in the room. Chuck was normally suspicious of such convictions unless they were backed up by rational thought. Moreover, the type of person they wanted was unlikely to be at a prayer breakfast – a young, ordained man, who could teach, would not mind long hours, had experience in prison, and who was preferably an ex-prisoner himself. Chuck could not, however, shake off his conviction, and eventually he told Paul that he wanted to say a few words.

What he said surprised the audience. He described the work that the Memphis chaplain would be expected to carry out and announced that he believed that the right man for the job was in the room. He asked him to come forward. As the meeting proceeded nobody came forward, and Chuck began to have doubts. Then, at the end, Fred Rhodes passed Chuck a card from a man who had written 'I may be the man.'

Bill Beshears had been imprisoned several times before he became a Christian. He later felt called to the ministry and was ordained. He then spent a number of years working with young criminals, and was also a teacher. He seemed a strong, steady

Christian, and had made a rededication to his faith after reading *Born Again* – he even wrote to tell Chuck about it. Chuck himself had added his name to the Prayer Breakfast invitation list, though he had forgotten all about it. Bill seemed perfect.

There was one major drawback, however. His family were well settled in Georgia and it seemed very unfair to uproot them. Chuck and Paul felt that he was the right man for the job, but did nothing to pressurize him. Bill and his wife promised to let Chuck know of their decision. A few days later Bill rang. They had talked and prayed about it and had decided that he should accept the post.

Bill was a popular choice with the prisoners, but other chaplains and the prison authorities were less certain. They were unsure about a chaplain from outside the system. They were even more uncertain about Jesse Ellis, a young black pastor who had been hired to help Bill. Again the inmates liked him, and he and Bill certainly made an impact on many men's lives. Yet the prison authorities regarded Jesse as a problem and eventually wanted to ban him from working in the prison. They believed he was preaching subversive sermons.

The sermon that had really caused the problem was about Paul and Silas in the prison in Philippi, when God broke down the prison walls and set the prisoners free. Jesse said that God would set the men in the Memphis prison free. The sermon was entirely scriptural and the prisoners loved it. Chuck turned to the prison warden and announced that this was just the sort of sermon that he expected his chaplains to preach. He explained the biblical references, but the warden looked unconvinced.

Prison Fellowship's work, it seemed, was in danger. Eventually Harold Hughes helped solve the problem in a speech at an annual meeting of prison wardens. Harold's speech was an impassioned plea for everyone to care for the prisoners. He talked of brotherhood, love and the healing of broken relationships through Jesus Christ. The audience was deeply moved and he sat down to rapturous applause. At the end several prison wardens came forward to express their support for Prison Fellowship, among them the warden of Memphis Prison. The danger was over, but it underlined the need for Prison Fellowship to learn to work with the system, not against it. Bill remained a popular chaplain among the prisoners, though Jesse later returned to his former position as adjutant of the Church of God in Christ.

Another important development that year set Prison Fellowship off on a new track. George Ralston, warden at the Federal Correctional Institution in Oxford, Wisconsin, refused to allow inmates out on furlough. Instead he challenged Chuck and Paul to bring a team into the prison and to run the course there. The Prison Fellowship staff did not think for one moment that Ralston was serious about letting them inside, but Fred suggested they take him up on the offer. If he refused, they could appeal to Norman Carlson and he would put pressure on Ralston to allow prisoners out for a seminar fortnight. Ralston called their bluff and invited them to go to Oxford prison three weeks later.

A little stunned by what they had rather unwittingly taken on, they set to work immediately. Ralston had allowed them a week in the prison. They knew that to spend a week there and then leave without giving the men any follow-up could be counter-productive. They needed local Christians to become involved and continue Bible studies and counselling afterwards. Like many prisons in the USA, Oxford Penitentiary was situated in an isolated area, making community involvement more difficult. Paul was set the task of finding twenty local volunteers, a task he knew would not be easy. Eventually, however, twenty-five volun-teers signed up, many of them happy to drive for at least an hour to reach the prison every day.

Prisoners signing up for the seminar were excused their normal jobs, and every effort was made to encourage them. Three days before the start date, however, only forty-six inmates had signed up (anything religious was regarded as suspect). Observers from other prisons, including several chaplains who had criticized Prison Fellowship in the past, were also planning to attend. Chuck knew that this could be an important turning point in their work.

Chuck was unable to attend the first few days of the seminar, since he had speaking engagements elsewhere, but Fred rang him to report on the first evening's events. He was ecstatic. Eighty-three prisoners had signed up and thirty local people joined the team to help. There was a marvellous atmosphere.

The seminar gained in popularity all week and by

the end about ninety-five inmates were attending, including a group of Muslims. One night, a Christian counsellor helping to run the seminar asked that anyone who wanted to invite Jesus into their hearts should raise a hand while he prayed. Hands shot up around the room.

The success of the first in-prison seminar set Prison Fellowship on a new track which it has followed ever since. By 1991 Prison Fellowship was working in forty-eight States in the USA and forty countries worldwide, and had presented its 5,000th in-prison seminar.

Many of the in-prison seminars have been memorable for a number of reasons. The second one which Prison Fellowship ever held was at Sandstone, Minnesota, the prison where Chuck and Dave Rolschau had been unable to find any Christians just eighteen months before. More men signed up for the seminar there than Prison Fellowship could cope with. This was also the beginning of a strong partnership with chaplain Norm Nissen, who had seemed relieved to see Chuck and Dave leave on their first visit.

Perhaps one of the most memorable seminars was a visit in 1978 to Atlanta Prison, Georgia. For two years the 2,000 inmates in that overcrowded prison lived under the threat of violence. Ten gangland-style killings took place in sixteen months, and beatings and fires were commonplace. Slim, one of the second seminar's trainees, had fled from Atlanta in fear of his life.

Jack Hanberry, previously chaplain at Atlanta in the 1960s, was appointed warden in the middle of all this violence. The prisoners immediately put him to the test by killing two men, assaulting several others and starting twenty-four separate fires. Paul telephoned Jack and offered the Fellowship's help. Chuck had some doubts about how safe it would be but, as Paul said, Atlanta was the sort of place that the Lord would want to go to.

There were just eight inmates in Atlanta's Christian fellowship, but the chaplain managed to recruit 150 men. Seventy-five of these later attended the seminar, the maximum that the facilities could accommodate.

The seminar took place one sweltering hot week, in just the sort of weather likely to cause a riot. Chuck joined them mid-week, and the evening he arrived he was due to give a talk. Before the meeting he joined the eight inmates from the Christian fellowship for prayer. They warned him that the atmosphere was very tense and that there could be some disruption. Nearly 1,000 inmates were gathering to hear Chuck. The Christians did not think that Chuck should talk about Jesus, but instead suggested he talk about prison reform. Chuck gulped. A thousand prisoners together in this angry, tense jail on a sweltering night – there was bound to be trouble. Hastily, after they had prayed together, he started preparing some notes on prison reform.

Between 800 and 900 prisoners turned out to hear Chuck that evening. They sat in an unresponsive mood as some of the Prison Fellowship staff talked. Then Chuck stood up. He did not know what to say, but he heard himself telling the men about Jesus.

The words flowed out of him, words he had not planned and which, he knew, had been put in his mouth by God. He told them of the history of Prison Fellowship, and of the love God has for the fallen and broken:

Jesus Christ came into this world for the poor, the sick, the hungry, the homeless, the imprisoned. He is the Prophet of the loser. And all of us assembled here are losers. I am a loser just like every one of you. The miracle is that God's message is specifically for those of us who have failed . . .

The message of Jesus Christ is for the imprisoned – for your families, some of them who aren't making it on welfare on the outside. Christ reached out for you who are in prison because he came to take those chains off, to take you out of bondage. He can make you the freest person in the entire world, right here in this lousy place.

Jesus, the Saviour, the Messiah, the Jesus Christ I follow is the One who comes to help the downtrodden and the oppressed, and to release them and set them free. This is the Jesus Christ to whom I have committed my life. This is the Jesus Christ to whom I have offered up my dream and said, 'Lord, I want to help these men because I have lived among them. I came to know them, I love them. There is injustice in our society, but we can change it. Yes, God, we can change it. I give my life to it.'[2]

As Chuck finished, dripping with perspiration and

exhausted, the room erupted. Men stood on their chairs, cheering and clapping, many of them in tears or smiling. The Holy Spirit poured out into that room and, though Chuck and his colleagues did not count the numbers, many men asked Jesus into their lives that night. Among them was a former Mafia man known as 'Joe the Butcher'. He called a dozen tough-looking men over to Chuck and in front of them did something he said that he had never done before. He apologized to Chuck for thinking that he was a phoney, and publicly asked Jesus Christ to come into his life. The following year almost 400 men were involved in chapel programmes in the prison.

Chuck did not want to leave the prison that night and he longed to stay with the inmates and his other Christian friends there. That night he had learned two vital things, and later wrote:

It was the ultimate for me in learning how to be used by God . . . Suddenly, so much came into focus right here in the most dreaded of all prisons: I really loved these inmates. These were indeed *my* brothers. It was here in Atlanta and in dark holes all across America that I experienced the richest, most meaningful fellowship. I could easily understand why Jesus went to people like these and places like this. Mysteriously and inexplicably, here one could sense the presence of God, the unspeakable joy of all joys.[3]

Notes

1 Charles Colson, *Life Sentence*, London, Hodder &
  Stoughton, 1979.
2 Ibid.
3 Ibid.

CHAPTER EIGHTEEN

Prison Fellowship Today

Chuck and Prison Fellowship were now firmly set on the path they would take in the future. The growth of Prison Fellowship has been steady and sure as thousands of people have become interested in the work. *Born Again* had a great impact on readers and when it was made into a film interest in Prison Fellowship escalated. Volunteers eager to help prisoners were signing up faster than they could be found work.

Prison Fellowship appointed seven regional directors to organize volunteers in strategic locations across the USA and in 1994 had fifty field directors. Local groups were given the responsibility of developing relationships with prison officials and organizing Care Committees to carry out a prison ministry locally. By the end of 1994 50,000 volunteers were involved. Befriending inmates in a number of ways, their involvement includes visiting individuals, attending chapel services and Bible studies, writing letters to prisoners and their families, and helping prisoners find work and housing when they are released.

Chuck never forgot the strain that prison life had imposed, not just on him, but on Patty and the rest of the family. Other former prisoners could also testify to this strain. Lee Corbin had wanted to escape from Maxwell when he thought that his marriage was in danger; Paul Kramer's first marriage ended in divorce. Statistics backed up Chuck's personal knowledge – the vast majority of marriages affected by imprisonment end in divorce. Prison Fellowship has therefore always stressed the need to help prisoners' families too, and many Care Committees are involved in supporting families. Prisoners' wives and husbands were always encouraged to join in the Washington discipleship seminars, but in 1981 Prison Fellowship took this a step further. A new training programme was started – now known as the Marriage Seminar – to give inmates and their wives or husbands an intensive week of Christ-centred marriage counselling. There are now also sixty 'spouse support' groups in the USA.

Perhaps one of the most touching aspects of the family work began the following year. Christmas is a particularly hard time for prisoners and their families. Not only are they apart, but the families on the outside often do not have enough money to buy presents for the children. The thought of children with no Christmas presents moved one woman to approach the volunteer Prison Fellowship Area Director for Alabama, Mary Kay Beard. Mary Kay was an ex-prisoner herself and she remembered Christmas in prison, when local church members brought in more gifts of soap and toothpaste than she could possibly use. She distributed them among other prisoners, and when the children came to visit their mothers at Christmas, many of them received a little gift of soap or toothpaste. Later she recalled,

'Can you imagine wrapping up a miniature tube of toothpaste and a bar of soap to give to your child for Christmas? Most children wouldn't think much of such small gifts, but in prison there was such joy on their faces! It didn't really matter to them what they got; it was from Mama.'

Mary Kay started a campaign to give Christmas presents to children on behalf of their parents in prison. As a result, 650 children received presents that year. The 'Angel Tree' idea – as it came to be called – so caught on that eleven years later, at Christmas 1993, nearly 363,000 children received Christmas presents and gospel booklets.

This is the story of one Angel Tree gift:

Some years ago a father named Jim bought two shiny, state-of-the-art, ten-speed bicycles: one for his son Jay, and the other for his daughter Sarah. On Christmas morning the children shrieked with excitement when they saw their gifts. They tore through the neighbourhood showing off their prized possessions. Sarah, more gentle, took great pride in caring for her special present.

The family scene soon changed, however. In 1983 Sarah was killed in a car accident. The house grew quiet, and the grieving family disposed of most of her things. They offered the bike to a cousin, who never came to pick it up. Jim tried to sell it at a garage sale, but no one bought it. The bike stayed in the garage, gathering dust.

Then in 1987 an inmate at Mississippi's Parchman Prison filled out an Angel Tree application for his daughter Ginger. Though she had had to make do all her life, Ginger had always dreamed big. She didn't know that you weren't supposed to ask for ten-speed bicycles on Angel Tree request forms, but she had wanted one for as long as she could remember.

A few weeks later, just before Christmas, the church's Angel Tree was explained at the Highland Methodist Church in Meridian, Mississippi. People eagerly clustered around the tree at the front of the sanctuary. Though he was caught in conversation, Jim kept his eye on the tree. The angels were disappearing rapidly. When Jim finally disengaged himself and rushed to the tree, there was just one angel left. The girl's name was Ginger and she wanted a ten-speed bike.

That afternoon Jim wheeled Sarah's bike out of the garage. It needed adjustments, a few new parts, and a good cleaning. With great care Jim overhauled the bike, rewrapped the handlebars and rubbed the chrome with a soft, clean rag until it shone. He proudly took the bike back over to the church. When he realized he hadn't checked the brakes, Jim hopped on the bike and took it for a spin round the car park, grinning all the way.

When church volunteers took the gleaming bike to Ginger on Christmas Eve, her face broke into a huge smile as well. The dream gift her dad couldn't deliver was hers – given by another dad who knew what it meant to lose a daughter he loved.[1]

* * * * * *

Lee Corbin was, of course, by no means the only ex-prisoner to find that it was all too easy to slip back into a life of crime. In fact ex-prisoners are the most likely group of all to commit crimes. Even those who are determined to go straight find the period after being released difficult and disorientating. Chuck himself had gone through a long period of uncertainty and readjustment after his release. In 1980 Prison Fellowship set up 'mentor matches' to link ex-prisoners and those about to be released with volunteers who will give them the support and fellowship they need to readjust to life on the outside, and to find homes and work. At the last count there were 2,300 mentor matches in the USA.

Five years after the successful launch of mentor matches, Prison Fellowship also set up Philemon Fellowships – support groups for ex-prisoners – and, in 1988, Life Plan Seminars. These teach prisoners near release practical skills such as how to set goals and manage money, and those needed for employment, friendships and leisure time. Other Prison Fellowship initiatives include Community Service Projects, whereby small groups of prisoners are given furloughs to stay with local Christian families and work on building renovation and maintenance projects; and Neighbours Who Care – a church-based pilot programme which began in 1990 – which aims to help the victims of crime regain a sense of security by giving them practical, emotional and spiritual support.

Another vital part of Prison Fellowship's work is Justice Fellowship, set up in 1983 and dedicated to improving America's criminal justice system. One of the most worrying aspects of the prison system in the USA, and elsewhere, is the severe overcrowding which leads to appalling conditions. Occasionally this boils over into violence and rioting. Justice Fellowship works with State and local officials to lessen overcrowding by setting up community service and restitution programmes instead of giving prison sentences to non-violent offenders. It also establishes in-prison work programmes and promotes victim rights.

Good ideas tend to spread and Prison Fellowship has been no exception. It has, in fact, spread to more than fifty different countries, and there are contacts in another forty-five nations. There are thriving Prison Fellowships in England and Wales, Scotland and Northern Ireland. The England and Wales Prison Fellowship was established by Sylvia Mary Alison in 1979.

Sylvia Mary's husband, Conservative MP Michael Alison, had met Chuck in 1974 before he was sent to prison, and Michael used to write to Chuck in prison. When Chuck later toured Europe in 1976, he and his family spent a few days with the Alisons in London. At the time Chuck was still working out his future, but he spoke to the Alisons about his vision for prisons. More than twenty years earlier Sylvia Mary had felt that God was calling her to work in prisons, however up until then, though she was ready to do so, she had had no opportunity. Uncertain of herself at the time, Sylvia Mary said nothing. Two years later she visited the USA, and Chuck arranged for her to join a Prison Fellowship team who were giving a seminar at a women's prison near San Francisco. Sylvia Mary had never been inside a prison before, but she found the whole experience remarkably easy. 'I felt so at home there,' she wrote later, '. . . totally identified with the prisoners and also at one with the visiting team. I felt that I could have spent the rest of my life there.'[2]

Meanwhile, back in the UK, other Christians were also thinking of a ministry to prisoners. Soon a group of them met regularly to pray, and eventually they invited Chuck to speak at a small conference in London in November 1978. Chuck was delighted to accept the invitation to speak and in the summer wrote to Sylvia Mary, clearly assuming that she and her friends were further on in their plans than they really were. This threw them into a panic and they turned to God in prayer. 'As we prayed,' said Sylvia Mary, 'the Lord gave us a picture of a house . . . a very big house [which] took in the whole of England . . . The ground floor of this house was the prison population and the people that the rest of society have cast off, and then the other floors were all the different sectors of society: at the very top . . . was the throne and the Crown.'[3] Then she felt God saying to them: 'Except the Lord build the house, they labour in vain that build it.' (Psalm 127:1) This house, Sylvia Mary believed, would be built through the prayers and works of Christians of all denominations throughout the country.

Prayer has been the sustaining force of Prison Fellowship in England ever since its launch in 1979. There are now 158 Prison Fellowship groups across England and Wales working with prisoners in 134 prisons. Prison Fellowship also started up in Scotland in 1981 after another woman, Louise Purvis, visited Corton Vale Prison. In words reminiscent of Sylvia Mary she said, 'I felt completely at home there. It was the first time I had ever set foot in a prison, yet I felt an instant identification with the women inmates.'[4] The following year, with the help and encouragement of Sylvia Mary, Prison Fellowship Scotland was born.

Prison Fellowship in each country is independent and each runs and finances itself. They are, however, all equal, and every year they each pay 5 per cent of their previous year's income to Prison Fellowship International. They all agree to the statements of faith and of purpose, and to use the same logo – the bruised reed, taken from Isaiah 42:3 'A bruised reed he will not break'. Prison Fellowship International acts as the enabling body, providing an overall source of inspiration and help. Every three years an international conference is organized to enable Prison Fellowship delegates from across the world to meet, share ideas and draw encouragement from each other. Accompanied by the ever-patient Patty, Chuck himself travels around the world, visiting prisons and Prison Fellowship groups.

Among the countless Prison Fellowship workers today is Rita Carroll, the UK's Northern Area Coordinator. As Rita Nightingale she spent three years of a twenty-year sentence in a Bangkok prison for her part in a drug smuggling operation. She became a Christian and was miraculously freed by Royal pardon. (Her story is told in *Freed for Life*.) Rita now visits churches and other Christian groups to tell them about Prison Fellowship and to encourage people to visit prisons and to care about prisoners. Every week she also visits Risley Prison for women.

She says:

Prison Fellowship is really about friendship, coming alongside prisoners. When I go into Risley I am obviously representing Prison Fellowship, but I go there as myself, just to see and talk to the women, to show that I care. I also try to encourage other people in the Church to do the same. I try to explain when I talk to a church group that caring for prisoners is more than just praying 'God bless all prisoners'; it's about befriending them and getting alongside them.

In general, I have to say that people in the Church tend to switch off if you mention prisons. Mention children and everyone wants to help, which is wonderful of course, but mention prisoners and it's a different matter. If you aren't a Christian and don't believe the Bible then fine, ignore them, lock them up and throw away the key. But if you do believe and you follow the Lord, you have to care for prisoners. Prisoners need help and friendship both in prison and afterwards. God could convert everyone in prison, but what would happen when they came out? There are some great Christian fellowships in prisons, but prisoners also need support when they are released. They need other Christians who can be sensitive to them when they go to church and give them support.

Over the years, Chuck's vision has inspired

thousands of people and helped countless prisoners and their families. Prison Fellowship is now the largest organization helping prisoners anywhere in the world. In recognition of this, Chuck was presented with the world's largest monetary prize – the Templeton Prize for Progress in Religion, worth £650,000. The prize was set up by Sir John Marks Templeton back in 1972 (just as the Watergate scandal was breaking) and is given in recognition of 'extraordinary originality in advancing human-kind's understanding of God'. When Chuck was told that he had won the prize, his reaction was 'not one of jubilation and exultation, but one of awe. I was literally driven to my knees, humbled and grateful to the Lord Jesus Christ whom I serve. I was both thanking God and asking him to equip me, that I would be a witness for him, given this remarkable opportunity worldwide.' He later added: 'Twenty years ago I was a broken man. I had the feeling that my life was over. To realize that God has used a broken life to reach out to hundreds of thousands of people is beyond me.' The prize, which Chuck requested to be given to Prison Fellowship as an endowment, was presented by the Duke of Edinburgh at a private ceremony in Buckingham Palace in May 1993. A public ceremony was held in Chicago the following September.

Chuck is undoubtedly the dynamo behind Prison Fellowship, although he would be quick to point out that he is just God's servant in this. Also, he stresses that he would not have started on this path without the support, love and prayers of his family and friends – Patty, Harold, Doug, Al, Graham,

Fred, Paul and Jackie – and many others, including of course Tom Phillips, who first told him of the love of Jesus. Other men and women around the world have carried out Chuck's and their own vision for the work. They all, however, recognize the vital part that Chuck has played in this. Sylvia Mary Alison recently described the Chuck she has known for many years:

Without a doubt, Chuck is the most energetic, dynamic man I have ever met. I remember feeling when I first met him as if I had been in the middle of a tornado, he brought so much energy with him. Patty, too, has great resources. She is marvellous for Chuck, an enormously funny woman who provides a great support for him.

In 1976, when we first met, he was full of insecurities because he was wondering what his life was for. He had started the prison work, but at that time he had not really got a focus. These days, of course he is more focused, and that insecurity has gone. But, looking back, I think that the insecurity in Chuck was like the grain in the oyster that becomes the pearl. The need to prove himself made him the sort of character he is.

He is still like a dynamo, even now almost twenty years later. He has had to slow down a little, but he is still more energetic than most people. He had an operation for cancer four or five years ago and suffers from diabetes, but you wouldn't know it if you met him. They caught the cancer at a very early stage and he is absolutely clear of it.

What makes Chuck a leader called out by God is that he has an enormous heart of compassion with a great love for the Lord and for the downtrodden. He is very affectionate, a large, tactile person who will hug anyone, male or female.

He is a highly articulate and intelligent man who is marvellous in interviews. He can answer anyone anything but is not pushed around. He can get across what he wants to say too – he doesn't let the interviewer dominate. And he can talk to anyone – Cabinet ministers, church leaders and prisoners alike, which few people can do.

Chuck is the founder and the flagship of Prison Fellowship worldwide. There has always been a great deal of prison ministry going on on a local scale around the world, some of it Christian and some not. The American gift and Chuck's inspiration has been to think big and to provide the technology required to draw the work together. Twenty years ago we in Britain didn't have much in the way of faxes and the type of technology needed to communicate worldwide. Nor did we have the big vision. Americans – and Chuck especially – have the energy that comes from belonging to a young country. He certainly helped us in Britain and woke up a lot of dormant, discouraged workers. And, for instance, in India, there was an organization which called itself Prison Fellowship. Prison Fellowship in America was able to look into it and then to draw the Indian group in with the worldwide organization, giving it extra encouragement and resources.

Chuck is the dynamo who started the whole thing off and who gave us and many groups the inspiration we needed to get going. One day of course, he won't be here any more and that will be a very sad day for everyone. But his work – Prison Fellowship – will carry on.

Notes

1 Prison Fellowship Ministries (eds), *Changed Hearts: Stories from the Ministry Founded by Charles Colson*, Washington DC, Prison Fellowship Ministries, 1989.
2 Sylvia Mary Alison, *God is Building a House*, London, Marshall Morgan and Scott, 1984.
3 Ibid.
4 Betty McKay and Louise Purvis (eds), *And You Visited Me*, Scotland, Christian Focus Publications, 1993.

CHAPTER NINETEEN

In Their Own Words

Perhaps the real testimonies to Chuck and the organization he founded should come from prisoners themselves. Here are the stories of two men – one from Scotland, the other from Cuba and later the USA – who have been helped by Prison Fellowship.

Eddie's story

'Eddie Boy' Murison was a rebel from the age of four when he realized that his stepfather did not want him. He was often in trouble, and by the age of nine regularly ran away from home. Eventually he went to live with his grandfather in Aberdeen, but again he could not keep out of trouble. Joyriding in stolen cars and stealing became some of his favourite pastimes. Even when he was sent to an Approved School he continued to steal and to run away. He also began to drink heavily, stealing alcohol whenever and wherever he could.

From his Approved School Eddie moved on to Borstal, then prison. He found it difficult to form stable relationships and already had one failed marriage behind him. He married again and had a daughter, but his wife decided that she had had enough and wrote to tell him so while he was in

Dumfries Prison. Eddie continues his story:

[The letter] was handed to me on Christmas Day by a prison officer with a smile on his face. Anger boiled inside me – partly against my wife, but against the prison officer even more.

My anger set me against everybody and I was just looking for trouble. I knew that one of the prison officers there drank a lot so I decided to 'do' him so I could get his drink. But every time I went for him, there would be another prison officer around. I attacked a 'con' [convict] who was walking past me, just because I heard from his accent that he was English – like my wife! I ended up in detention where I fought with the three prison officers who came to take my clothes.

After a week or two in the detention cell the chaplain, Bill McKenzie, came to see me. He said that God had sent him to help me. 'This is a joke,' I thought, and I told him so.

'God loves you,' he said. He went away then, but left behind a leaflet called *Journey Into Life*. I couldn't really read or write as I had never attended school for any length of time, so I had never read any books. I thought about what he'd said, picked up the leaflet, then threw it down again. Later that day I picked up a book called *Hooked* by Ernie Hollands, an ex-prisoner. For the first time in my life I read a book right through. Then I got the leaflet and read it through. I didn't know at the time, but God was showing me how to read!

At six o'clock that Friday night [14 January 1987] I asked Jesus Christ to come into my life. For the first time in my whole life I felt good, really good. I knew God had started something good in me. My attitude towards 'cons' and prison officers changed for the better. I felt that, because I was a Christian, I had to start being good towards other people. For the first time ever, I began to accept the system instead of fighting it.

With just a few months of his sentence left, Eddie was moved to Glenochil Prison. Here he felt out on a limb and scared he might forget his new faith. However, the Prison Fellowship group there supported him and helped him keep hold of his faith.

One day my life was in danger. Four guys were all 'tooled up' and out to get me. I had only weeks left to serve, and I remember saying to the Prison Fellowship couple, Frankie and Eddie Macguire: 'If you really believe in God, pray that nothing happens to me.'

The next day I walked over to one of the guys and took his knife from him. 'God doesn't want you to do this,' I said. The four guys ended up in my cell and I found myself speaking about the love of God and what he could do for them. We met a few times in my cell after that and talked about Christ and what he was doing in my life. The Bible says 'If God is for us, who can be against us?'

On 12 October 1987 I was released from prison and went to stay with Eddie and Frankie Macguire from Prison Fellowship. I knew that they understood the new life I had started with God and I knew they would be able to help me. While staying with them I went through a deep spiritual experience. I felt my old life being washed away and I was filled with a new life. I had heard this could happen, but it was wonderful to experience it for myself.

Later I returned to Aberdeen to live. I found a good church, which I still attend. At first I found it hard to mix with people: I thought they were all snobs. But thanks to the people in Prison Fellowship, I have gradually started to open up more as a person. God used Prison Fellowship to help me get rid of some of my old hurts and learn to trust people for the first time in my life.

Eddie felt that God wanted him to help feed Aberdeen's many homeless and so started to take them soup and blankets at night. Soon he was running Outreach for the Aberdeen Needy – OFTAN – from his church, providing homeless people with food, washing facilities and a change of clothes. He often talked about Jesus and what God could do for these homeless people. He says, 'I've seen really hard men in tears as God reached out to them. It is beautiful to see the changes that come upon people's lives when God touches them.'

Eddie married again, this time a Christian

woman, and together they have become involved with the Prison Fellowship group in Aberdeen. He also found a steady job with British Rail. Eddie stresses, however, that life is not always easy and straightforward, even for a Christian ex-prisoner.

After all the troubles of my earlier life, the hardest fight for me was to stay a Christian once I got outside. All the temptations were just looking at me wherever I went. I am learning to trust myself to stand by my commitment to God and to trust other people to help me get through my change of personality. It's a hard struggle sometimes.

When I look back, I see God's hand in my life and how he used Prison Fellowship to pull me out of the wasted life I was in. God had plans for me. He reached out to me when I thought I would not be good enough to be a Christian. He showed me how to put my old life behind me and go for the new life he had planned for me . . .

It hasn't all been straight going, though. About six months after my release I fell flat on my face with drink. I had got drunk and ended up in a fight and really hurt a guy. That night I went on my knees in prayer before God and asked him to help me to stop drinking and doing crazy things. Then I opened my Bible and read Isaiah 51:22. I knew that God meant them for me: 'This is what your Sovereign Lord says, your God, who defends his people: "See, I have taken out of your hand the cup that made you stagger; from that cup . . . you will never drink again." ' I have never taken alcohol since that day.

Prayer is the way I ask God for help, and he has never let me down. I know I've come a long, hard road, but Jesus has given me the best life. He carries me at times when I feel I can't keep going. In prison I had given up, but then God came in and showed me the way out of hell. Prison was hell to me, but through the chaplain and Prison Fellowship, God renewed my mind and set me free. He still comes this way for guys like me, if they will just realize that Christ is the only way out – if we are to stay 'out'.[1]

Omar's story

The squeeze was tight. On 16 May 1980, 250 refugees from Cuba crowded onto a shrimp boat made to hold 125 – maximum. Like most of the other emigrants, thirty-year-old Omar Gonzales had abandoned everything – family, friends, job – to chase the elusive dream of freedom. The political refugee spent the night retching into the choppy sea, praying he'd make it to Key West. He'd tried to escape his homeland three times before. Omar knew the ache of defeat. But finally, shortly after dawn, he spotted pelicans on the horizon, then a beach. This was it.

As Omar walked down the gangplank, a uniformed immigration officer handed him a Coca-Cola – as if it were a prize or a symbol of the good life to follow. That afternoon, Omar and the other 125,000 emigrants sat under government tents, gorging themselves on hot dogs and crisps. 'It was a tremendous feeling of plenteousness,' says the Cuban exile. 'You could serve yourself as much as you wanted. In my country everything is strict, the food is rationed; it was really a shock.'

A few days later Omar boarded a government plane bound for Fort Chaffee, Arkansas. While in flight, he employed his broken English to translate for the crew and passengers. He was happy to be of service in his new land.

After forty-five days in the tent compound he tracked down and convinced the one American he knew – a batchelor he'd met at a Hemingway fishing tournament – to sponsor him. No longer living under the threat of deportation, Omar moved to the Virginia suburbs of Washington, DC.

Working as a labourer and part-time bartender, Omar soaked in the opulence of his new land. Having subsisted in Cuba on three-quarters of a pound of meat every nine days and five pounds of rice per month (plus what he could get on the black market), he wandered supermarket aisles in amazement. How could he choose one brand of bread out of twenty? It was all too much, too soon. 'I went bizarre trying to replace twenty years of communism in one year,' says Omar. 'Having never been in a democracy, I didn't know how to handle myself.'

He especially didn't know how to handle credit cards, the seductive tempters of the good life. They embodied the American dream, the ability to have anything he and his new wife wanted. Having established credit by purchasing two cars, he was courted by MasterCard, Diner's Club and American Express. He took up their magical offers and charged away his life – enjoying a fancy stereo, expensive jewellery and lavish vacations. With plastic wands he pursued his idea of freedom – the freedom to feel important. 'I was Mr Rockefeller,' he says. 'American Express offered me a $15,000 credit line – it was incredible. When they send you a card like that, you have to use it.'

But eventually Omar's dream turned into a nightmare. He visited a fellow immigrant early in 1984 and, overcome with a debt of tens of thousands of dollars, asked how his friend afforded his luxurious lifestyle. The answer? Cocaine.

Convinced it was a harmless drug, Omar began selling and using it. 'I used to go to parties where they served marijuana and cocaine on silver plates. At one point I started believing drugs were legal because they were everywhere.' As he became enmeshed in drug trafficking, however, Omar realized he was snared in a deadly trap. The people – and their white powder – were dangerous. 'Something inside of me was saying, "Get locked up and get out of this mess."' When an undercover agent threw him to the ground and stuck a gun to his head, Omar was terrified, yet oddly relieved.

Six months after entering the drug world, Omar sat in a county jail staring at a Bible someone had handed him. He remembered his youthful days in the Roman Catholic Church before Castro came to power, and his teenage years handing out tracts for an underground Church. 'I didn't really know Jesus personally; I just liked the risk.' More recently, he had lost his university teaching post in Cuba and narrowly escaped imprisonment for telling one student he thought God had created the world. Now, as a criminal with his back turned to God, he had been *given* the outlawed book. 'It blew my mind away,' says Omar. 'I thought if you were a convict, a drug dealer, you were of no worth. That Bible symbolized a love I had never experienced.'

Feeling deserted by his wife, with no friends or family near, he was lonely. 'God, I'm nothing,' he said. 'Nobody cares about me.' A year later, in the autumn of 1985, Omar attended a Prison Fellowship in-prison seminar at the Virginia State Prison where he was serving time. 'I was drawn by the poster with people holding hands,' he says. 'I kept seeing those clasped hands, their unity.' At the seminar Omar met Prison Fellowship volunteer Jimmie Massie, a stockbroker turned farmer. As their friendship developed through Prison Fellowship Bible studies and visits, Omar became secure in God's love through his people. 'In prison I felt guilty about how much damage I did to teenagers, businessmen – who knows? – but I took all that guilt to Christ and left it there.'

Omar was paroled after serving three years in prison. He was given a change of clothes and $80. 'I couldn't have made it without Jimmie, or someone with his love, concern and willingness to risk,' says Omar. 'He and other Prison Fellowship volunteers gave me capital and a place to live. They provided encouragement when I needed it most.'

They also taught him to make – and stick to – a

budget. His first two pay cheques went towards debts that had been outstanding when he was jailed. The godly discipline Omar learned in prison and the relationship he developed with Jimmie helped him once he gained freedom. This time he could handle its responsibilities. 'I learned in prison to trust God for everything, to put Christ first in everything.'

Three months out of prison, Omar began teaching high school equivalency classes to prisoners near Richmond. Although ex-prisoners are rarely allowed into prison so soon after release, Jimmie convinced the Department of Corrections (DOC) of Omar's skill and integrity. As one DOC official acknowledged, 'Our business is trying to re-establish people in the community, to give them a chance to rebuild their lives. We ought to be right in it ourselves.' Omar was thrilled to be used as Christ's instrument, to bring love to a place of great need. 'It was a dream come true to go back and let them know by my walk – not my talk – that Jesus remakes you, that you don't have to live in crime.'

Omar also got part-time work at a hospital for drug addicts. Having been a prisoner of the State – and of drugs – he commands the respect of those still captive. 'Today I'm able to say something I wasn't able to say before, that I am concerned and I *love* you. I see transfigured faces when I say that. Until Prison Fellowship, nobody ever confronted me and said, "Omar, I love you."'

'America is no longer America where I'm going to be rich,' says Omar. 'Today I enjoy people a lot more. And would like God to use me to reflects his love to other people.'

He also understands liberty better. Having lived under communism, where life was threatened, and capitalism, where the pursuit of happiness led to despair, Omar has found true liberty in Christ. 'Freedom today,' he says, 'is the freedom of worship, the freedom of fellowship, and the freedom to express myself toward the One who created me. That's real freedom.'[2]

Notes

1 Eddie's story is extracted from Betty McKay and Louise Purvis (eds), *And You Visited Me*, Scotland, Christian Focus Publications, 1993.
2 Omar's story is quoted from *Changed Hearts*, Washington DC, Prison Fellowship Ministries, 1989.

Acknowledgements

The author acknowledges with thanks permission to use the following material:

Direct speech quotations on pages 1, 17, 22, 46, 50, 53, 54, 56, 57, 59, 63, 65, 67, 68, 78, 80, 81, 90, 91, 103, 107, 108 and 119 taken from *Born Again*, by Charles Colson, London, Hodder & Stoughton, 1979.

Direct speech quotations on page 114 taken from *Blind Ambition*, by John Dean, New York, Simon and Schuster, 1976.

Direct speech quotations on pages 120, 123, 128, 129, 132, 135, 142, 147, 150 and 158 taken from *Life Sentence*, by Charles Colson, London, Hodder & Stoughton, 1979.